LEARNING
TO
BREATHE

LEARNING TO BREATHE

RACHAEL NEWHAM

spck

First published in Great Britain in 2018

Society for Promoting Christian Knowledge
36 Causton Street
London SW1P 4ST
www.spck.org.uk

British Library Cataloguing-in-Publication Data
A catalogue record for this book is available from the British Library

ISBN 978–0–281–07808–0
eBook ISBN 978–0–281–07809–7

Typeset by Fakenham Prepress Solutions, Fakenham, Norfolk NR21 8NN
Manufacture managed by Jellyfish
First printed in Great Britain by CPI
Subsequently digitally printed in Great Britain

eBook by Fakenham Prepress Solutions, Fakenham, Norfolk NR21 8NN

Produced on paper from sustainable forests

For my mum, who has been there for every breath

Contents

About the author

Rachael Newham founded the Christian mental health charity ThinkTwice in 2010 after visiting mental health inpatient units throughout Hertfordshire as part of her degree course. She completed a research master's entitled 'Towards a Contemporary Pastoral Theology of Clinical Depression' at the London School of Theology and now spends much of her time travelling the country preaching, speaking and writing about issues related to faith and mental health. Rachael lives in Hertfordshire with husband Phil, lots of books and Phil's bicycle paraphernalia! She blogs regularly at www.rachaelnewham.com, while drinking lots of coffee and indulging in her love of photography on Instagram.

Acknowledgements

There are more people than I ever imagined involved in writing a book; and many people without whom I would have been unable to write.

Thanks are due first to Juliet and the rest of the team at SPCK for wise, gentle, encouraging edits and a beautiful cover!

Second, to the faculty and staff at the London School of Theology for helping me to shape the beginnings of my theology of mental health and providing much encouragement along the way.

Third, to the staff at St Peter's in Harrow for letting me write in their office, use their printer ink and providing much needed light relief when I was writing the tough stuff.

Fourth, the Maxted family. Writing a book about mental illness can be harrowing at times and their friendship, humour and sofa space has been invaluable.

Fifth, to Simon, who has taught me so much about pastoral care, not only in his pastoral care of me but also as I've watched and shadowed him professionally.

Thanks also to my wonderful family and friends; Dad for supporting me through two degrees and beyond, Virginia, Grandma, Grandpa for believing in me before I could believe in myself, my in-laws for welcoming me into the family and my friends for their encouragement and fun throughout the process.

And finally to my Philip, who put up with lots of evenings alone while I wrote, coped with crises of confidence, cheered me on and makes me laugh every day. Thank you and I love you.

Prologue

It begins slowly, so slowly that I hardly notice at first. My chest tightens and my heart starts to beat a fraction faster.

I try to draw breath, but instead I choke on oxygen I can't inhale.

As I realize that I can't breathe, the panic wraps itself around my mind.

I can't make myself draw a breath.

Tightness snakes around my brain and I feel the blood racing through my veins.

Not again.

I try to catch my breath. It feels as though I've been holding my breath for hours and I begin to shake violently, my foot connecting with the floor as it taps out a strange rhythm.

I see the world as though underwater; sounds are dulled and my sight is blurred.

And then suddenly I'm breathing as fast as I can, trying to suck all the oxygen from around me, trying to claw my way back to reality.

I know I'm breathing too fast, but I don't feel I can control it; there's a rushing sound in my ears and pins are prickling my fingertips. I try to attract the attention of someone close by. Despite feeling this way countless times before, I'm scared. Maybe this will be the time I don't catch my breath.

I need to breathe. I need to find someone to help me.

I need to come back.

I search my foggy brain for a way to ground myself, but before long I've stopped breathing again. It's as though there is a scream lodged in my throat, pressing itself into my voice box, and I am silent as I gasp for breath.

I'm gasping for air again, hoping someone will remind me how to breathe.

Introduction

This wasn't the book I intended to write.

I've been writing stories for as long as I can remember, from childhood ramblings about mummies and daddies, via the macabre Plath-esque stories of misery that populated my teen years, to the blogging and freelance articles which have become such a huge part of my job since leaving university.

I thought I would write a theological tome or a memoir of missionary adventures. I expected to be in my sixties, writing in my retirement about a working life full of daring adventure. I didn't expect to be writing a book on suicide and depression in my twenties. It often feels a little strange to be writing any kind of memoir when I'm not even in my third decade, but I take comfort from the fact that God uses unexpected people in unexpected ways; from the shepherd boy chosen to lead an army, to the teenage girl chosen to carry the Son of God in her womb.

Despite high-profile campaigns and pledges, there are few conditions that provoke as much scorn as mental illness. I hear countless stories, both online and offline, of jobs lost and relationships ravaged by invisible illnesses that some prefer to believe don't exist, and it's not a problem from which the Church is exempt. So often, the Bible is used to shame those struggling with the most common of mental health conditions. For example, 'You can't have depression because the Bible says you need to be full of the joy of the Lord', or 'You can't have an anxiety disorder because it says "Do not be anxious" in the Bible.'

I can't remember a time when I wasn't a Christian: my faith and the Church have been part of my story since my first breath. It began with the prayers of a five-year-old concerned about burglars and the Rwandan genocide (in that order) and has continued so that I now spend my life writing about faith and visiting churches to talk about the gospel, which shines even in the darkest corners of the human mind.

I believe the gospel has something important and healing to say, not only to the one in four of us who lives with a mental illness each year but also to the countless more who watch their friends and family members battle diseases that consume their hope and vitality.

I'm sharing my own story, but I also want to look again at ancient stories, sharing the hope and challenge I've found in their words. A number of passages have spoken to me over the years: the darkest of the psalms, which seems to contain no glimmer of hope in its verses; Elijah atop Mount Horeb, fleeing for his life before begging for death; and the scriptural silence on the day hope was buried in Joseph's tomb with no light of resurrection in sight.

It can't stop with the retelling of ancient stories, however; there is action to be taken here and now in our churches to help them become places of sanctuary for those seeking refuge.

I can claim no expertise in mental health other than the knowledge gained from copious reading on the subject and over a decade living under the shadow of a mental illness. But from the shadows, I've seen God move – often not in the miraculous flashing light of healing, but instead in the days when his strength was all I had, and in the actions of those I love who, on countless occasions, have poured themselves out for me.

This may not be the book I intended to write, but I hope that, as you read it, you will catch a glimpse of the God who is with us in every breath.

1 First breaths

As someone who is now pathologically early for everything, it always strikes me as ironic that I arrived almost two weeks late. I was born in the middle of a heatwave, facing the wrong way and took nearly three days to make an appearance and take my very first breaths.

My mum recalls that the first time she held me was in a cupboard, as there was no room left on the ward, while my dad tells me that when he left the hospital that night without his wife or baby daughter he shed a few, very rare tears.

It was perhaps not the most auspicious start.

The first days passed, however, with the photos and hospital visits common to many babies born all over the world. Photograph albums annotated with my mum's beautifully written captions show a small dark-haired bundle being cradled by various family members and friends of my parents.

It soon became clear, however, that all was not well in my tiny body. I was unable to feed and had a piercingly high-pitched cry, accompanied by a rapidly rising temperature. As I dropped nearly a pound below my birth weight, I was admitted to the special care baby unit at Whipps Cross hospital. The two weeks that followed were filled with confusion and a battery of tests, not to mention agony for my parents and wider family and friends as this tiny little human seemed to be getting more and more unwell.

The medical team treated me for various possible ailments, including meningitis, prescribing me antibiotics and performing two lumbar punctures and countless other tests as they desperately tried to work out why on earth my temperature kept rising.

At some point in those first weeks I had a neonatal fit. A brain scan showed that I'd had a cerebral haemorrhage, causing fluid on the brain. It was an answer to the question of what was wrong, but it wasn't the one everyone had hoped it would be.

The whole of my church family was praying, my name appearing in the faded newsletters my mum has kept in my baby box. There are stories that give that period a light-hearted slant, though, from the feeding tube I insisted on pulling out every five minutes to the bald patch and cup on my head, there to administer medication, which made me look like a monk.

In the midst of those days, my mum became a woman of prayer like never before. She prayed with the fervency of Hannah praying for Samuel all those thousands of years ago. It's described in 1 Samuel 1.26–28:

> and she said to him, 'Pardon me, my lord. As surely as you live, I am the woman who stood here beside you praying to the LORD. I prayed for this child, and the LORD has granted me what I asked of him. So now I give him to the LORD. For his whole life he shall be given over to the LORD.' And he worshipped the LORD there.

In her prayers, just as Hannah did, she offered my life back to God, for him to do with what he willed, and hoped that she would be able to bring me up. It was a brave prayer and a powerful one because, before I knew anything of her prayer and its significance, I knew that my place in the world was to be found in some kind of Christian ministry. It's easy to think that somehow this was an expectation I grew up with, but I never experienced it like that. My faith grew as I did, but I had no comprehension of how it had been sown right at the beginning of my life.

I find it hard to understand the enormity of what my parents went through. I know that these things happened. I know my small, very new body was put under a great deal of pressure. I know that the legacy of those early weeks marked me, not only physically but also mentally, in ways I can't imagine. I can't possibly know the trauma of watching your daughter fight for life at only a few weeks of age, but I do know that it marks a family in ways that resound through the years.

When I finally came home, just shy of a month after I was born, life began. I was sent home with the warning that some damage had been done to my brain, but they couldn't be sure what it was. They knew my motor skills were unaffected but they didn't know what the seizure and swelling had left in their wake. My parents bought me brightly coloured educational toys they could ill afford in order to stimulate my brain and ensure that I would grow up 'OK' – whatever that means. Despite weekly and then monthly visits to the hospital to have my head measured and anticonvulsant medication every day, I had the kind of life that a million children in the 1990s did – full of bright clothing, Disney princess regalia and play dates.

There was a lurking anxiety beneath the surface. I was physically weak, and countless episodes of bronchitis and breathing difficulties saw me return to hospital on more than one occasion for steroids and antibiotics, with an eventual diagnosis of asthma when I was just over a year old.

A psychiatrist would note many years later that I had grown up with a sense that my body could not be trusted. It hadn't occurred to me before I read his words, but it is true. When you grow up with a chronic illness such as asthma you learn caution. You're cautious about how much you challenge your body, cautious in terms of making sure that you always have your inhaler, checking if you're wheezy enough to tell your mum, how tight your chest is. These things didn't stop me enjoying my early childhood, but they did make me aware, very early on, of my limitations.

Despite the lurking health difficulties, my first memories are happy, of times spent with my family and my church. I'm an only child and our close-knit family was a bedrock of support. When Mum went back to work, I was often looked after by my grandma. They were golden days; I attended a nursery I loved and I was growing into a confident child.

One of my favourite pastimes was pretend cooking. At home with Mum I watched her cook, helping her with my small hands as she made my dinner; and with Grandma I did the pretend stuff. Grandma would line up the ingredients I was allowed to use, usually a combination of instant coffee granules, dried spaghetti and flour. I would spend hours making concoctions, proudly serving them up as lotions and potions. Grandma's garden was a wonderland, covered in ivy with a pond holding countless koi carp (eventually joined by my goldfish), which I would proudly feed on Grandpa's behalf.

Then every year, when summer rolled around, so would the annual church holiday club. I loved it because I got to spend time in my favourite place with my favourite people. And the year when I was five, in the aptly named 'upper room' at my church, we were asked if we wanted to say the commitment prayer.

I'd never experienced a time when I hadn't thought God was real, but as I prayed that prayer, something in me clicked. I had the most tangible experience of the Spirit moving through me. I knew without doubt that this Father God was someone I wanted to get to know better and I knew that I could trust him.

We sang a song about being safe in the Father's hands and I felt a swell of love, pure and uncomplicated. It wasn't a dramatic, Damascus road conversion experience, but a quiet realization that I was created by God and loved by him. That realization changed everything – not because I was leaving behind a sordid life of difficulty (I was five, after all!) but because I was beginning to gain confidence.

I also became aware, through the wonders of CBBC *Newsround*, that there was a world outside my safe home. The genocide in Rwanda had happened a year before and I calmly announced to my assembled family (and later to half my church) that I wanted to be a missionary there. This dream lasted for a while before I realized that Rwanda is definitely not close enough for me to get back for dinner at home every night! From then on, however, I was almost certain that I would work for the Church in some way or other. While I vaguely entertained the idea of being a teacher, a singer or an actress (sometimes all at the same time), I always returned to the knowledge that I was going to do something for the Church.

For a long time I felt as if my conversion story was somehow deficient. There was nothing dramatic about a five-year-old promising to follow God for ever; the sins I repented at that age were far from heinous. Throughout my primary school years I gave talks about my infant faith at school and spoke about Jesus all the time. I also asked at least once a year to be baptized – but was repeatedly told that I was too young.

When I was ten, however, I stopped asking.

It was a few weeks into the new millennium and my dad came to pick me up from school. It was a rare treat, as his job in a hotel often meant he worked long hours, getting home way after I was in bed. That day I skipped happily along beside him, slightly perturbed by his silence but happy nonetheless.

When I arrived home, however, the reason for Dad's silence was revealed. Mum was in the lounge, face pale and eyes red-rimmed from crying.

'Rachael. I'm really sorry, angel, but Uncle Den died today.'

I stared at her, unable to comprehend what she was saying. Den was one of my grandparents' best friends and he and his wife lived in a bungalow by the sea. We'd spent many a happy hour with them, even as, over the past few years, Den had grown frailer and been confined to his armchair.

I didn't know how to deal with the grief I felt at his death and the sadness I felt for his wife, Rita. I began to ask, for the first time, where God was in this.

Where had God been in Den's last days?

Where was God for his wife and all of us left behind?

They were questions I dared not voice, but they nonetheless dampened my faith. I didn't stop believing in God, but I stopped seeking him.

Ironically, the year that followed was one of the happiest of my life. I loved being in Year 6 and I loved singing the lead role in the end-of-year show. I felt confident and happy.

The photo albums show me proudly posing in my new oversized school uniform; but as the summer wore on, I began to feel increasingly anxious about starting 'Big School'. There seemed to be countless things to worry about: getting my homework in on time, finding my way around the maze of different buildings, making sure that I had all the equipment I needed in order to avoid my great fear – detention.

On the first day, I met the girl who would become my best friend. I was seated alone in the large English classroom, feeling breathless and disorientated as everyone else paired up. The teacher, Mrs R, seemed to be the sort who took no nonsense and I was afraid of her. Fifteen minutes after the start of the lesson, a girl came in shyly and quietly apologized for being late, explaining that she had gone to the wrong class. Mrs R waved her excuse away and gestured to the empty seat next to me. I shrank into the wall, unsure of what to expect from the pretty girl beside me, her bright blue eyes framed by the curliest eyelashes I had ever seen.

Around halfway through that first lesson, we became friends. Spotting a poster of Winnie the Pooh on the wall directly in front of where we sat, I smiled to myself and gently gestured to Jessie, as she had introduced herself. A giggle emanated from her body like bubbles in a bath and we became firm friends. A loose group of other friends formed around us and I began to feel if not comfortable, then certainly more settled at school.

When the new minister, Simon, and his family came to our church, his daughters also became great friends of mine and I threw myself into the opportunities afforded me by being a member of the youth group. I sang regularly in the worship band and, after one particular youth service, I found myself praying again the commitment prayer I had first prayed at the age of five. It wasn't that I had ever stopped being a Christian, but the questions I'd had about where God was when life hurt had felt like a block, preventing me from really committing to him.

I grew in confidence and was happier at school. When, in February, I attended the baptism of a couple of close friends, I was in tears even before the service began. Everything I read and heard both before and during the service stirred something in me that made me feel that I should be baptized.

I was 12 years old and the sermon was on the story of the raising of Jairus' daughter. Mark's Gospel gives us Jesus' words to the girl, *Talitha koum!* (which means 'Little girl, I say to you, get up!') For perhaps the first time, I felt that words from Scripture were speaking directly to me. Jairus' daughter is believed to have been 12 at the time the story took place and I, being the same age, felt that the words applied to me. After asking so often to be baptized and being told no, I felt as though this time God was asking me to 'get up' and be baptized, to start a new life.

After the service I approached Simon and Mum and prayed with them. Simon agreed to baptize me a few months later, once I turned 13. Perhaps this was my first lesson from God that his timing is better than ours (it's a lesson I'm still to learn many years later!)

The day of my baptism proved to be everything I had hoped. I was filled with overwhelming peace as I declared my love and commitment to the Lord in front of everyone I knew and loved. The gnawing sense of calling I had first felt at the age of five was further strengthened by the many scriptures, both written in the numerous cards I received and read to me by members of the congregation during the service, that spoke of me taking the word and comfort of God to others.

Although only 13, I knew that my future lay in the Church. It would take me much longer to work out exactly what that future looked like.

2 Struggling for air

The word 'depression' is so commonly used that it easily loses its potency. The British weather is said to be 'depressing'; people claim to be 'depressed' at the state of the world. My husband says he's depressed when QPR loses at football (which happens a lot). Yet none of these situations bears much resemblance to the reality of clinical depression. It's had many guises over the centuries, from the melancholia described by Hippocrates to the sin-induced malaise it was believed to be in the Middle Ages, until it was finally recognized as a psychiatric condition in the nineteenth century.

Depressive illnesses include conditions such as seasonal affective disorder (SAD), dysthymia (mild but persistent depression lasting for over two years) and post-natal depression. While the main symptoms are the same, they differ in the ways in which they're experienced and their causes. SAD, for example, is governed by the seasons, with some people experiencing their symptoms in the darker winter months and others during the summer. Post-natal depression follows the birth of a child and can, contrary to popular belief, affect both the mother and the father.

Some types of depression might have relatively obvious causes, but there is no single cause of depression. Instead it's far more nuanced and includes a whole range of differing factors, from a family history of depression to physical illness, stressful life events, such as divorce, or drinking too much.

Sometimes depression is caused by going through a difficult life experience: a significant change, such as getting married or moving house, losing someone you love, or a difficult childhood that might involve neglect or having a parent with a chronic illness or all kinds of other difficulties. It can be almost impossible to locate a single cause of someone's depression; more often than not lots of different causes combine to lead to someone developing depression.

It's important to remember that I can only write about my own experience of depression, and my experience is far from definitive (see Appendix). Many people may experience some or all of the symptoms of depression at any one time. Also, depression isn't simply about the presence of symptoms – it's about how those symptoms affect the reality of life for a sufferer. It tends to be thought of as either a medical phenomenon or a passing phase – these are the two extremes of people's perceptions of what depression is and how it affects those with a diagnosis – but the reality is that it is much more than its medical definition and more entrenched than a passing phase.

It's hard to describe how depression feels. It's unending grief and terror, blankness and a sense that you are experiencing the world through a dirty lens – everything is dimmer and murkier. The overwhelming experience of depression for me is one of exhaustion. Sleep is never enough to lift the tiredness that seeps into every cell of my body, making every step feel as though I'm trudging through lead.

John Swinton, Professor of Theology at the University of Aberdeen, writes:

> As one reflects upon the nature of depression it becomes clear that it is a profoundly spiritual experience that cannot

be understood and dealt with through drugs and therapy alone. Its central features of profound hopelessness, loss of meaning in life, perceived loss of relationship with God or higher power, low self-esteem and general sense of purposelessness, all indicate a level of spiritual distress.[1]

The range of symptoms that can present as part of depression are as varied as the people who are afflicted by it. Some may find their movements become laboured and slow, while others experience restlessness and racing speech. These polar opposites also exist in terms of sleep. Some, like myself, find sleep a constant struggle, running the gamut of early morning waking, disturbed nights and nightmares. For others, wakefulness never happens – their eyes are impossible to open and their body feels like it's filled with lead, difficult to get out of bed.

Whichever way the pendulum swings, however, the unrelenting exhaustion remains. For me, disrupted sleep is usually the first sign that I'm getting ill and, for those we support, it's worth working together to figure out how depression affects them and note the early signs of struggling.

One of the defining symptoms is anhedonia, which is the inability to enjoy things that used to give you happiness. You find that the things which would usually give you pleasure no longer lift your mood. It might be a lack of interest in reading, sport or shopping, but this dulling of joy can make you feel like life is very far from the promises of Jesus when he declared that he was coming to bring life to the full. It's perhaps among the most paralysing of symptoms, for one of the first things we might do when we're feeling low is try to comfort ourselves with things we enjoy, yet anhedonia makes this near impossible.

During periods of depression I found that I had to develop new ways of passing time. Reading tired me out too quickly and going out filled me with anxiety, so I began to make a scrapbook of happier times. I watched endless reruns of *Friends* on DVD and began filling in colouring books (they didn't have adult colouring books at the time so I had to make do with Disney princess ones!)

The defining aspect of depression is not just the symptoms it evokes but also the way in which these symptoms affect your ability to live your life. The symptoms themselves may occur in many of us, but it's when they begin to interfere with life that a diagnosis of depression may be made. A diagnosis not only involves the presence of anhedonia but also takes into account how symptoms affect the sufferer's ability to function in everyday life for at least a two-week period. The disruption of everyday life can be hard to come to terms with and there's no way to prepare someone (or those around that person) for the way in which depression storms through life. It makes the best days of your life feel like a distant dream and the worst days feel like an inevitability.

Learning how to live with and around depression is not something you can achieve overnight. For many of those early years I dismissed people's assurances that learning to cope with my feelings would make me feel better; but there was certainly much truth in it.

It's hard to pinpoint when depression became an unwelcome guest in my own life. There had certainly been shadows for as long as I can remember – times when thoughts became clouded and tears fell fast, times when, as a young child, I recall feeling an inexplicable sadness that usually resulted in spending playtimes alone singing Céline Dion ballads – but the idea that I was actually ill didn't emerge until I was 14.

The preceding year hadn't been particularly eventful. School had been difficult – I had had a few arguments with my friends, a distant uncle died. These things weren't easy, but they certainly weren't catastrophic. There was nothing that I could pinpoint to explain the fog that seemed to be filling my mind.

I can clearly remember walking around my garden, trying to hold back the tears and wondering if I had depression, before chastising myself that I was too young for that and I was being melodramatic. It was a thought that would return and be dismissed numerous times before I finally sought help, and a further five years before I was given a diagnosis.

The summer before I began my GCSEs, I went on a Christian holiday camp with a few of my friends from church. I wasn't well suited to what was planned – a week of outdoor activities, a hike and a night sleeping in the open. I was, and still am, an indoors kind of person.

In the week before the camp my anxiety grew and I think I cried from the moment I arrived until the moment I saw my mum again at the end of the week. On the surface it was homesickness; in retrospect it was a week-long panic attack and when I returned home, I still felt uncomfortable. When school began a few weeks later, I cried again, every day for two weeks. Never one to embrace change from choice, I found the new classes and pressure of being a GCSE student paralysing. I couldn't explain what was going on in my head, other than an overwhelming sense of separation and isolation.

I spoke to my favourite teacher, Mrs B, who had taught us Religious Studies since Year 7 and was universally adored. Her bright blue eyes were kind and they pierced my own tear-filled ones. She helped me get through each day and I regularly found refuge in her office, with its tissues for my tears and sneaked chocolate biscuits.

My church was another place of refuge for me. To use a biblical word, I felt the community offered me a vision of shalom. 'Shalom' is often interpreted as peace, yet it is something far greater and more nuanced than that. Theologian John Wilkinson describes shalom in the following way:

> The root meaning of the word shalom is wholeness, completeness and well-being . . . It does, however, have several second meanings encompassing health, security, friendship, prosperity, justice, righteousness and salvation, all of which are necessary if wholeness, completeness and well-being are to come about.[2]

Shalom is a vast concept and, much like everything God-given, it's outside our comprehension. Yet shalom is intensely practical as well, as are the things that are provided for Adam and Eve in Genesis: love, safety, food and drink. These things are the bedrock of human life and are set out in Genesis as ingredients without which we cannot flourish. As the Church, we need to learn from this passage as we respond to those with mental health issues. We are not called to be mental health experts, psychiatrists or psychologists; we are called to be bringers of shalom and witnesses to the hope that comes from heaven.

Genesis 2 goes into more detail, telling us that Adam and later Eve had beauty and an appreciation of beauty (v. 9), boundaries (v. 16), companionship (v. 18), work (v. 19) and freedom from shame (v. 25). Some of these are the very things that the

World Health Organization outlines in its own definition of mental health as 'a state of well-being in which every individual realizes his or her own potential, can cope with the normal stresses of life, can work productively and fruitfully, and is able to make a contribution to her or his community'.[3]

Our mental health is far more than a lack of mental illness, and the passage in Genesis shows us that; it shows us wholeness. While the phrase 'mental health' doesn't appear in the Bible (which was to prove somewhat problematic for me when writing my dissertation on the topic), what we do have is shalom: God's perfect vision for mental and physical health that we will one day experience in its fullness.

Although the initial awfulness of school faded when I was able to swap some classes around, the crying didn't stop completely. I cried every single week at church. Throughout the songs, through every youth session, tears fell unchecked down my cheeks and I didn't understand why.

Never before had I cried with such regularity, my body convulsing with wave upon wave of sobs that seemed to express something I was feeling but did not understand. I spoke to my youth pastor and the minister of my church, probing where the tears were coming from. I clung to the promise of Revelation 21.4 with a ferocity that I had never before needed. In the sea of endless tears, I had to believe that there would be a day when 'He will wipe every tear from their eyes. There will be no more death or mourning or crying or pain, for the old order of things has passed away.'

We still feel such shame about crying. Often tears are seen as the ultimate sign of weakness; they conjure up images of weeping willows and Victorian ladies overcome with the vapours. Yet we read in the Bible that it was through tears that the people of Israel lamented their exile, it was through tears that Jesus grieved for his city and it was through tears that the risen Lord was first seen. And let's not forget the shortest verse in the Bible, found in John's Gospel. Two words: Jesus wept.

That is something startling to me, even now, many years after I first read the verse. The king of heaven and earth shedding tears in Jesus' humanity. It's such a beautiful picture of Jesus' love for Lazarus breaking his heart. Hearts don't break over things they don't love, and Jesus' tears were not only for his friend but also for creation in all its frailty and brokenness. Luke 6.21 reads, 'Blessed are you who weep now, for you will laugh.' I hoped desperately for a time when I could laugh, because my friends didn't understand why I was crying and I didn't know how to explain that I couldn't explain it.

I felt like the friendships that had been solid were faltering as I withdrew into my head, sick of who I was becoming. The nagging adolescent discomfort within my skin grew and morphed into a hatred that I carried around with me. It grew as I did, and the more people told me that I was precious and worth investing in, the more it hurt, as if I was holding in something disgusting that would make everyone run from me.

I thought they were merely being kind, that they couldn't see what I could. I felt like I had a layer of respectability covering something foul and hateful. I began to convince myself that I didn't deserve God's love. I was given readings of Psalm 139:

For you created my inmost being;

you knit me together in my mother's womb.

I praise you because I am fearfully and wonderfully made;

your works are wonderful,

I know that full well.

The words, uncomfortably familiar, became acutely painful. I managed to twist each word and phrase that was meant to build me up so instead I could justify my self-hatred. I didn't understand how I could be a Christian and feel so low, so I thought I must be a bad Christian, because Christians are meant to share the joy of the Lord and I didn't see how I could do that when I was crying all the time.

I don't think it was ever explicitly expressed to me, the idea that you had to be happy to be a Christian, but I equated joy with happiness. I wanted to tell people about Jesus, but I didn't think crying was a particularly good witness. In my desperation and guilt, I studied the Bible like never before. I clung to the verses I'd been given by my friends and my youth worker, trying to squeeze as much hope as I could from the words.

One that was given to me quite early on was from Paul's second letter to Timothy (NKJV): 'For God has not given us a spirit of fear but of power and of love and of a sound mind.' Paul was Timothy's pastor and he writes to him here in such a tender and caring way. Verse 4 says that Paul recalls Timothy's tears and that brings to my mind the shepherd of Psalm 23 leading his flock home.

It's a vision for what good mental health can look like and it is something I've returned to time and again in the years that have passed since. I didn't want to be afraid of life, I didn't want to hate myself, I didn't want to feel like I was losing my sanity.

The words offered me a hope to fix my eyes on when all else seemed hopeless. Power, love and a sound mind were what I craved. Power over my emotions, so that they wouldn't overwhelm me day after day; a sense that I was worth something, anything; and the ability to feel as though I was in control of my own mind and heart and could work out how to deal with emotions without destroying myself in the process.

As the school year drew to a close, things improved a little. I was enjoying my friends again and looking forward to my fifteenth birthday. Then came July. Within the space of three days, my uncle was told his cancer was terminal, my best friend Jessie's dad was diagnosed with cancer and London was attacked by terrorists.

It's interesting – as a psychiatrist would observe some years later – that none of these things affected me directly. My dad worked in London and, after the attacks, wasn't able to leave the hotel he ran for several days, but that wasn't particularly unusual. I was devastated for Jessie and sad about my uncle, but each event was a step removed from me. They seemed to confirm everything I'd feared since the beginning of that year, however – that life got worse as you got older. I felt as though life would never be better than it was now and I wanted something to relieve the pressure in my head. I wanted to be able to see something of the turmoil that resided there.

Notwithstanding this, on the day of the London bombings in 2005, I sat in the bath and stared at my shaving razor. The sharp metal was seductive. I wanted to draw it across my skin. I wanted the relief that I was sure would follow. I lay the edge there, resting the blade against my skin before stroking it across my middle. I had a clear sense that I wanted the pain to stop; I wanted a relief that tears could no longer provide. Beyond that, I'm not sure what drove me to press the razor deeper and pull it across the skin I held taut between two fingers.

For a few weeks I'd been wondering what it would be like, sometimes getting as far as lightly grazing my skin but stopping short of making a cut. This time, however, three shallow slits appeared in my skin and a few seconds later the beads of blood collected and formed into shockingly red lines. I stared at them as I sank beneath the water to wash the blood away.

My skin stung, but my mind was silent for the first time in what felt like years. It was the silence that shocked me at first as, for so long, I'd had thoughts clanging through my mind relentlessly and now, nothing. I moved slowly as I gathered myself together to leave the bathroom, revelling in the new-found quiet.

Within minutes, I was staring at myself with disbelief, unable to connect the sting on my abdomen with the fact that I'd inflicted it on myself. Guilt seeped through me, as though someone was pouring it down my throat, setting it alight. How could I have been so stupid? How selfish and disgusting. What had I done?

I don't think I understood that I had just self-harmed. I felt disgusting and guilty, but despite knowing what self-harm was, I didn't connect the two; I just got on with the business of hating myself.

I found myself drawn back to cutting throughout that summer, although I'm not sure how often I turned to it. I know that it felt wrong and bad, but it gave me a legitimate reason to hate myself and feel punished. It calmed my thoughts, if only for a few moments.

I researched cutting and self-harm countless times over that summer. Then, as now, I read to understand, to ease my panic and help me to grasp the workings of my own mind. I didn't consider it an act of violence, because I didn't value my body enough to think that hurting it mattered.

All my life, my body had been an inconvenience. It didn't look the way I wanted it to; didn't fit into my friends' hand-me-down Gap jeans. I couldn't run without wheezing and coughing and I didn't seem to have the immune system to fight off even a cold. Self-harm, unconsciously, became a way to punish my body for not working in the ways that I felt it should.

As the new school year rolled around, I began to feel anxious once more. I had arranged to do my work experience placement at a hotel in the same group as my dad's. I started to cry uncontrollably again, all the way into London on the train, holding back the tears all day at work before crying all evening.

One evening as I sat in tears, my mum looked at me with something akin to terror in her eyes.

'When you feel really bad, do you ever hurt yourself?'

My breath caught in my throat as I nodded my wordless reply, unable to say 'yes'. She pulled me into her arms and held me as I cried for a long time that night. I could tell she was upset and I felt even more wretched. Not only was I hurting myself but I was also hurting my mum – the person I loved most in the whole world.

Church remained my refuge. I still cried through most of it, but I couldn't wait to get back to the place I felt safest. I was often there four nights a week: helping out at the Monday night kids' club, cell group on a Tuesday, prayer meeting on a Wednesday and youth group on a Friday before church again on Sunday. Church was my life, and I've often thought back to those years and realized that I probably loved church more than I loved the God of the church.

When Jessie's dad died that December, I clung to church even more desperately. The day after he died, we went to visit her. It was the first time I'd ever heard her house silent – grief hanging in the air like smog, making it hard to breathe. Jessie clung to us and we listened to her, unable to understand the depth of her loss, each of us trying to be the friends she needed us to be.

When we left her house, shocked by the cold air, I begged Mum to take me to church, where an Advent service was taking place. I crept in at the back and howled, repeating again and again that I wanted to die. I didn't want to do this life, which hurt me and those I loved so deeply. The people I was with looked on helplessly before praying with me and encouraging me that I was needed in this life, that Jessie needed me. It was what stayed my hand that night: I knew I couldn't possibly leave this life when my best friend had just lost her dad – it would be too selfish. So I decided that I would live because Jessie needed me to live and because my mum loved me. They were doubtless good reasons to stay alive, but they became for me an obsession that would continue for the rest of the year.

After a difficult Christmas, I'd been persuaded by my mum and my pastors that I should really see a doctor, and I'd convinced myself that I'd be in a locked ward by the end of the day. I didn't know how to even begin explaining everything that was going on in my head, and I dreaded the doctor asking to see the marks of my despair.

I'd chosen the youngest doctor in the practice, for no other reason than I liked the look of her, and she was brilliant. She listened to me speak, encouraged me to open up and pointed me to further help. Over the next few years, Dr T would be a constant in what seemed like a revolving door of mental health professionals. She arranged for me to go to a local children's counselling project, which I did a few weeks later.

I'd begun to panic about it pretty much as soon as I got the letter. I remember having to tick a box on the assessment form saying 'thoughts of self-harm and/or suicide' and feeling like a fraud. The questions about whether or not I'd ever been violent to others made me shudder. I felt like I was a criminal being condemned for a crime I'd committed against myself.

When we pulled up to a large residential house on a street not far from my school, it wasn't what I'd been expecting. I think I'd imagined it to be far more clinical. Instead, there was a ramshackle scattering of plants in the front garden, with weeds poking through the paving stones and the door painted in a chipped pillar box red. I stared at Mum as we knocked on the door and it swung open to reveal a tatty hallway and a woman smiling at us.

The woman, lovely as I'm sure she was, seemed to me a caricature of someone from the Jacqueline Wilson novels I'd devoured as a child. Her glossy red lipstick also covered most of her teeth and she wore a bobbly pink jumper with rainbow-striped tights. She spoke in a sickly soft voice as she ushered Mum and me along the corridor, which smelt of oven chips and sweat. We were shown the small kitchen, where a boy was baking cookies, and passed various other rooms painted in various primary colours that barely disguised the battered walls. The room we eventually stopped at was painted green, with a few office chairs and a few more brightly coloured beanbags that had seen better days.

Mum and I sat awkwardly side by side as the woman began to talk, the same weak smile laced with something that looked like pity remaining on her face and her voice breathy, as if she were talking to a small child. I sat, mute, feeling every part of me the moody, uncommunicative teenager. I tried my best to explain what had been happening over the preceding months and years, but the words seemed to get stuck between my throat and my mouth. When she asked Mum to leave us alone for a while, I recoiled. The idea of being alone with this woman made my skin crawl. I sank further inside myself, barely even caring that I was being rude. I wanted to get out as soon as possible.

When we left, I shook for hours. I refused to return, refused to have any sessions, refused to explain why I wasn't going back. To be honest, I wasn't sure why my reaction was so violent, but I knew that I wanted to have nothing to do with the place again.

And so the year continued. I kept talking to my pastors and found myself in my head of year's office regularly. In fact, so frequent were my panic attacks and tears that she kept a *Friends* DVD in there to give me time out if I needed it. Mrs Y was brilliant and as ferociously devoted to her Year 11s as a lioness. She was strict and would take no nonsense, but she was also incredibly maternal and I owe her a huge debt of gratitude for getting me through my GCSEs.

My friends tell me now that I preferred the company of small groups and hated eating in public at the time, so some days I was lost to them behind glazed, tear-filled eyes. In truth, I can't remember much of that time – I see it through a fog, with only vague shapes visible that are impossible to reach. Elizabeth Wurtzel, author of the seminal book *Prozac Nation*, wrote one of the best descriptions of depression I've ever come across: 'That's the thing about depression: A human being can survive almost anything, as long as she sees the end in sight. But depression is so insidious, and it compounds daily, that it's impossible to ever see the end.'[4]

As May of that year arrived, I lost hope completely. My sleep had always been erratic, but I now no longer slept properly at all. I was awake for hours each night, sleepwalking through each day, and I started crying again. The tears fell unchecked all day and when they dried up, my body heaved with silent sobs. By Thursday, after three days spent in Mrs Y's office, alternately crying and catatonic, she sent me home mid–morning. I remember Mum coming to collect me and tucking me into bed as if I were very small again. Finally, I slept.

I remember tearing through the pages of my Bible, desperate to find some comfort in its words to cling to. Time and again I was drawn back to the Psalms: they expressed something in me that I couldn't articulate, especially then.

Psalm 88 has been called the saddest psalm. Its words are unrelentingly sad and express both how depressed people can feel in themselves and seem to others. It is a psalm that has no resolution, no reminder of God's steadfastness amid the pain. Indeed, the only hopeful reference comes in the first line: 'Lord, you are the God who saves me; day and night I cry out to you.' The hope lies in the declaration that God is God and the acknowledgement that in him lies salvation, and that he remains present and loving, even when we feel at our most unlovable.

It was the honesty of the psalm that captured my imagination and heart, I think. Walter Brueggemann writes that this psalm 'is an embarrassment to conventional faith'.[5] It is not the image people want to portray in their churches: it has no ultimate celebration, no triumphant confession of faith. Yet it spoke particularly to me as I fought constantly to hide behind the smile that I felt was expected of me.

The Psalms stand against the empty 'I'm fine, thanks' expressions that are regularly exchanged in every church across the land. When I felt unable to connect with anyone else in my life, I started to be honest with God, even while hiding behind my smile when faced with anyone else.

I remember being surprised the first time I read Psalm 88 that it had no resolution. The psalm's final words weren't 'Praise God' or anything remotely worshipful. Instead, it concluded, 'Darkness is my closest friend.' Not only was that how I felt but also the very inclusion of it in the Bible gave me, and continues to give me, great hope.

My diary at that time was filled alternately with age-appropriate discussions about my latest crush and desperate prayers about the fact that I didn't know how to go on. My GCSEs passed in a blur. My only clear memory of that time is my maths exam, which was preceded by a panic attack so disruptive, I was given special consideration. It has struck me a number of times since that it's possibly the only reason for my having a maths GCSE – God really does work in strange ways sometimes.

There were spells of happiness that summer. The pressure had lifted and I spent most of the time with Jessie at her house, reading and chatting under the huge trees in her garden. In retrospect, those were golden days – all the more precious because we knew that, at the end of the summer, Jessie would be moving to Devon. My commitment to care for her, to stay alive for her, was at the back of my mind and I didn't know how I'd cope when she left. Still, we pushed aside our worries and enjoyed picnics, twilight barbecues and a great deal of singing in one another's bedrooms. The spot on the horizon was results day, which felt almost cosmic in its importance. It had been billed as the pinnacle of our lives so far and I switched between dreams of achieving certificates full of As and A*s (with probable Cs for maths and science) and nightmares in which I failed the lot.

When I walked into school to collect the long-awaited results, I felt trepidation, but not panic. I knew that I couldn't have done anything more. Surrounded by my friends, I opened the envelope and withdrew the two sheets of paper I believed would determine the rest of my life. Excited shrieks surrounded me as friends congratulated each other on papers littered with As.

As I stared at my own, I heard a rushing noise in my ears. My eyes pricked and I forced myself to hold in a howl. I felt I had failed. I hadn't even got an A for RE, my favourite subject and the one I was best at. In retrospect, they were perfectly good grades, a mixture of Bs and Cs, with an A in English, but I was devastated.

I walked out to Mum's waiting car and collapsed in tears as she tried, rather puzzled, to find out what my grades were. Mum was thrilled and proud. After all I'd been through in the last two years, it was miraculous I'd managed to get any GCSEs, let alone some good ones! We'd meant to go and celebrate, but all I wanted to do was cry, so we went home and I cried out my disappointment.

Eventually I pulled myself together. I was hosting the results party that evening for my friends, complete with Bacardi Breezers and Smirnoff Ices. I wanted to be happy for all they'd achieved and so I went out with Mum to Café Rouge – although the only thing I wanted to celebrate myself was being able to do the A levels I'd chosen.

That night's party was fun, but at the back of my mind sat one word: 'failure'. I had done worse than any of my friends and I could tell they were tiptoeing around me so as not to rub my nose in the pay-off of their hard work (or, in some cases, very little work). After about three hours of wearing a painted smile, I was tired and excused myself to go to the toilet.

As I sat on the toilet seat, I put my head in my hands and glanced at the razor sitting on the side of the bath. It beckoned to me like drugs beckon to an addict needing a fix. I picked it up and, shaking slightly, held the razor to my leg. The metal was cold, even though it was a warm night. I drew it across my skin just as I heard a shout of laughter from the other room. I jumped and the razor tore at my skin, the blade going much deeper than I'd intended. I frantically ran around the bathroom trying to find something to stop the bleeding. It was morbidly comical, hearing my friends enjoying themselves next door while I tried to stem the steady stream of blood running down my leg. It worked, though. I felt connected again and I knew I would be able to get through the evening with a smile on my face.

Once I had cleaned myself up, I returned to my room and the partying carried on. By the time everyone had left and

I was picking up glasses and bottles from the floor, my leg was really throbbing.

In the days that followed, I sank into a deep depression. I stayed indoors, wanting to avoid everyone's questions about results day, not wanting to hear the congratulations that I didn't feel I deserved. As far as I was concerned, I was a failure and no one could convince me otherwise. In fact, it would be a number of years and two degrees before I would be able to feel proud of my GCSE results. Whether that's an indictment of my own pride or of an increasingly pressurized education system, I'll leave you to decide.

Starting sixth form was something of a revelation. For the first time in years I began enjoying school. I missed Jessie and I felt low, but I loved my lessons and the freedom that being a sixth-former brought. I particularly relished no longer having to sit through maths and science! At the same time, however, I became convinced that my life wasn't going to last much longer. I was exhausted – mind, body and soul – and with the knowledge that Jessie was settling into life in Devon I couldn't see the point of carrying on. The promise I'd made myself almost a year before to stay alive to care for her seemed redundant now.

The self-harm, which until that point had been something I did only in moments of crisis, was becoming something I relied on. I was cutting nearly every day and it seemed to be losing its effect. My mind looked for something else – something that would make some kind of difference to the pain I was in – and the only conclusion I could reach was that for the pain to end, my life had to end.

The more I self-harmed, the less I could cope without my macabre method of self-soothing. I was calmed by the process, by the knowledge I'd been punished and by the dressing of my cuts as I prayed that as they began to heal, I would perhaps feel something in my heart heal too.

As autumn approached, on one of the coldest days of the year so far, I felt something in me snap. I would later learn to call it dissociation, the sense that I was cut off from my body and out of others' reach. As I walked through school that day, I passed Mrs Y and she stopped to speak to me, as she often did. I can't remember now what I said to her, but I remember her tone of voice and it was one I hadn't really heard before. She sounded almost scared, and she decided that I needed someone to speak to. As I sat in her familiar office later that day, still lost in a haze, Mrs Y told me that she was going to introduce me to the school chaplain, so that I could have some support to get me through the year.

Al, the chaplain, was a youth worker from New Zealand with boundless energy. While I'd seen him around, I was terrified at the prospect of him seeing the worst of myself before I could present the showreel I usually played for people. In the end, though, the story fell out without much effort. I was sitting with my friend Rebecca in the Christian Union meeting and she asked me how I was doing. Unbidden, tears filled my eyes and she led me by the hand next door to Al's office.

'How are you?' he asked, a small, sad smile playing across his face. 'Stupid question, I guess.'

He steered me to a seat as I started crying again and slowly made my mouth form the words to describe how awful I was feeling. I remember that it felt as if a bottle of cola was being painfully unscrewed.

Slowly, I choked out how much I was cutting and how much I hated feeling so bad all the time, but how it was a relief too. There was a sense that something was shifting in me. As I spoke, I realized that I didn't have much fight left and I wasn't sure what was to come.

I ended up returning to Al's office countless times and those hours taught me a great deal about pastoral care. He pointed me to a hope that I couldn't see and barely believed in, that God uses our darkness for his illumination. He encouraged me to stop hiding behind my façade and be honest with myself and those around me about how I was feeling. They are lessons I've held very dear in the years since, both as I manage my own mental illness and as I walk alongside others.

A few weeks after our first meeting at the Christian Union, I stood outside the school's 'Holy Hut', where Al had his office, and looked at the laughing teenagers scattered across the car park, the younger ones queuing up for a breaktime sausage roll.

This would still all happen if I died.

It was, in my mind at least, a turning point. The realization that life would continue without me – people would still laugh and everything would move forward – allowed me to think that if I took myself out of the equation, people would get over it and would be happier without me. For the first time, perhaps, I seriously considered taking my own life.

3 Suffocation

The first time the words 'I want to die' floated through my mind, I can't have been older than six. I was at school and I don't think anything more distressing had happened than being left out of some activity by my friends. I don't remember being shocked or distressed by the thought, but I do remember my thoughts quickly moving from death to a trip out with my mum the following week. For as long as I can remember, then, dying had been an option, and I remember thinking of it as a way out long before I needed one.

I wasn't, at that point, actively suicidal. I didn't want to die and I certainly wasn't considering a time or a place; it was simply an option. This passive thinking about suicide wasn't the same as the active suicidal thoughts I would experience that November, over ten years later, and, if I'm honest, it's not something that I found particularly troublesome at that point in my life. Passive thoughts about suicide still need to be attended to, however – the idea isn't something that, if voiced, should be ignored, because it can become active.[1] Also, as my depression began to take hold, there was a shift in my thinking. Even when I'd first voiced the words after Jessie's dad died, I wasn't sure that it was really what I wanted and I had no plans. As time went on, though, I found my thoughts lingering on suicide more often than they had when I was a child.

And so the realization I had that November day wasn't shocking to me, but it was the moment the idea of suicide stopped being passive and began to be a very real wish to end my life. It seemed almost logical to end my life before it could get any worse. Year on year, life had seemed to get harder, my depression more intransigent. Adulthood was a terrifying prospect.

Later that day I sat again in Al's office, tearing a piece of tissue to shreds, my hands shaking. The realization I'd had scared me and all of a sudden I wasn't sure if death was the answer. I wanted desperately to tell someone about the fear and ambivalence I was feeling about continuing my life.

'I don't want to do this any more,' I whispered as the tissue disintegrated between my fingers.

'Do what?' Al replied, looking at me with what I now recognize was fear.

'I don't want to live. I want to die.'

Al let out a long slow breath.

'This is bigger than I can deal with alone.'

I started to shake violently, my foot hitting the floor so hard I could hear it beating a tattoo. Tears began to fall, although I wasn't crying. The shock of saying the words out loud made me realize how serious I was. Although I had considered it many times before, and thought about it many times since Jessie's dad died, this felt different. I think Al sensed a resolution and resignation in my tone that hadn't been there before.

As I left school that Friday afternoon I knew I was going to have to face this in a new way. I needed to tell Mum about the meeting Al had arranged with the deputy head, who was in charge of safeguarding, to talk about what happened next. I avoided the subject until Sunday evening, and once again I saw the pained look in Mum's eyes – she knew there was something that I wasn't telling her.

By Monday my bravado was at its peak. I put some make-up on to cover the dark circles beneath my eyes and decided to present myself as 'struggling, not desperate'. Ms H, the deputy head, was a fierce woman, tall with severely cut blonde hair and a no-nonsense attitude. She wasn't someone who invited confidences, and I was incredibly grateful that Al accompanied me.

I can't remember a great deal about the meeting itself, but I do remember thinking in the back of my mind that I was obviously a good liar as I presented Ms H with a version of myself that would sound like I wasn't constantly walking the thin line between dealing with life and deciding on death.

It was at this point in my life that I first became aware of how important the language we use around mental health issues is. For much of the meeting the rhetoric referred to my self-harm as 'doing something silly', and feeling I wanted to end my life as 'doing something stupid' or 'committing suicide'. Suicide hasn't been a crime in the UK since 1962, yet we often still use criminal language when referring to it. You commit a crime; you don't commit suicide. In recent years there has been a positive shift towards understanding that the language of suicide needs to reflect this reality. We now use wording such as 'completed' suicide, rather than 'committed'; 'incomplete' suicide as opposed to the phrase 'failed suicide attempt'. Language such as 'doing something stupid' is not only incredibly patronizing, but also stigmatizing. Self-harm and suicide are neither silly nor stupid; they are expressions of something inexpressible, ways of communicating hopelessness. I can still recall that, on leaving the meeting, I felt as though I were a naughty child, an inconvenience, rather than a young woman desperate for someone to take my inexpressible pain away.

Two days later, any vestiges of wellness I'd cobbled together had disappeared.

That morning had been the year's first Advent service. Spirits were high and we all enjoyed the irony of Al leading an Advent service when he'd never even attended one before. I remember laughing in his office with my friends, perhaps a little too shrilly, before heading off to my lessons.

It wasn't until lunchtime that the switch went in my head again. I was sitting with Rebecca and her boyfriend, and although included in the conversation I felt as though I was floating above it, unable to connect with what was being said. The feeling wasn't uncommon to me, but it was frightening nevertheless – to be at once in the world and completely unconnected with it. The years before this moment had been more difficult than I could have, or would have, ever imagined. Mental illness had me firmly in its grip and I was getting too tired to continue the fight.

I had grabbed a strip of paracetamol that morning because of a headache, and as I sat, barely hearing the words spoken to and around me, I gently pressed the crispy silver covering of the packet and popped the powdery tablets into my mouth. I can't really say what I thought this would achieve. All I knew was that I wanted the pain and pressure in my heart to ease. My chest hurt, almost as if my heart really was broken. Paracetamol is a painkiller and my mind could see only that. My headache that morning hadn't been a bad one, but the ache in my heart and soul was almost unbearable.

We had PE all afternoon on a Wednesday and I managed to ignore my crashing heart for the first hour, despite my mind's focus on the rest of the tablets sitting in my jacket pocket. I pulled off a skilled acting job, pretending I was fine, while I tried to get my brain to formulate something nearing a plan. I was sick and tired of being alive but not living – of being so lost in my head and my pain that my thoughts couldn't and wouldn't stray from self-harming, from taking some more painkillers.

The next hour was to be spent in the fitness suite. I sat on the shiny wooden bench in the changing room, the air heavy with sweat and Impulse body spray. I can picture it so clearly even now. I pulled the rest of the packet from my bag and stared at the white plastic against the beaten and battered varnished wood. It seemed so stark. I took more. This was it. I could end my life with my next move. I could feel myself falling far away from reality, until . . .

'I think I should look after those, don't you?' came Rebecca's voice. I tried to protest, but my mind was unable to form the words fast enough and I before I knew it the packet had been whipped out of sight and I was being dragged back into the fitness suite, where I could have 'an eye kept on me'.

I pounded the treadmill with a ferocity that I didn't believe I possessed. It was the fastest I'd ever run and certainly faster than I've run since. My mind had homed in on my one focus. I wanted to die. Nobody was going to stop me. What had started out as one horrific fortnight had lasted far too long. Everyone said that the teenage years were the best of your life – but if depression, self-harm and exhaustion were the best life had to offer, I was sick of it. My thoughts were racing. I quickly realized that in order to achieve my aim I would first have to calm down, and second I would need to convince Rebecca that I had a headache and I needed the paracetamol to relieve it.

Somehow, I pulled myself together and managed to convince her to give me the packet. She insisted on watching me and kept asking me, again and again, if I was sure I hadn't already taken some. It was at times like this that I discovered I could be a consummate liar. This isn't something to be proud of, merely a sign of the utter desperation that was raging through me – I was on a one-way road to self-destruction.

I didn't want any unnecessary distractions.

Standing before her, I quickly swigged back the tablets with a glass of water. Then I shot back into my body and my heart was flooded with fear. I had no concept of how much paracetamol is lethal and as I realized I might just have begun to kill myself, the primal instinct of self-preservation swung into action. It was as though the proverbial switch had been flicked in my mind again and I snapped back to reality.

Rebecca asked me once more if I was sure I hadn't taken too many. This time my body wouldn't let me lie and I shook my head before I could stop myself. She asked for a third time, and again my head reacted with a shake before I could do anything to stop it. What had felt so sure for me, so final, now seemed uncertain.

What about my mum?

As the question entered my mind I was floored. How could I have done this to her? How could I have been so selfish? Why was I such a horrible person? Mum loved me, even though I was a pathetic excuse of a daughter and I was throwing my life away. I didn't deserve death – it was a cop-out. I didn't know what to do with the desire to die that sat so firmly next to the pain and selfishness of what I had just done. What if I was going to die and people who took their own lives weren't allowed in heaven? Was I going to hell?

Before I could finish the thought, someone grabbed my arm and pulled me towards Al's office. I remember what happened next in the third person. I had drifted far out of my own head and all my recollections of that day from here on in flash through my mind like stills from a film, badly edited and jarring.

Seeing Al walk down the steps from his room, on his way home, I couldn't look him in the eye. He fired questions at me, none of which I can remember answering. The next thing I was aware of was that I was being led to the medical room with Al saying, 'I'm not asking you, Rach, you're coming to the nurse's station.'

Rebecca, Al and I reached the medical room and I sat down, unable to think past what I'd done and unsure of what I wanted. The voice of the school nurse broke into my thoughts as she entered the room.

'You're not meant to be here, you know? You should have come to reception.'

I watched her face fall as Al explained what had happened. I gathered that Ms H was being summoned. Rebecca disappeared, and Al left, having told me something I have no memory of.

I sat next to the nurse and she said to me that many years before, she had sat in a similar place, wanting it all to end. She told me her story with incredible gentleness, encouraging me that life was worth fighting for. I felt calm for the first time that day; then, just as I began to wonder what was going to come next, Ms H swept into the room and started speaking at great speed.

'What have you done? We're going to need to get your mum and she'll have to take you to hospital. You'll probably have to stay to be assessed and you might need your stomach pumping. They might not let you go home; you might be sectioned for your own safety as you've tried to commit suicide. Your mum's on her way in from the car.'

I cowered and shrank into myself, wishing only to disappear. I felt sick.

Mum entered the room, ashen faced. I can barely imagine the agony she must have been feeling at that moment.

She drove me to the hospital in near silence, only pleading with me to stay awake. I desperately wanted to sleep.

I sat down, still dazed and unable to focus, as Mum went to check me in. It wasn't long before I found myself in a cubicle, and a nurse with kind eyes and a shock of red hair came and sat on my bed.

It was her kindness that pierced the fog. The guilt pushing its way into my mind had blinded me to my mum's love and care that day, but this stranger was the one who broke through. I can't remember what she said to me, but I do remember squirming as I showed her my most recent cuts. The marks of my despair were so deeply private that it felt like I'd been exposed.

After I'd been seen by the nurse and had blood tests, we were taken back to the waiting area and we sat watching *Neighbours*. It was surreal, such normality in the midst of such extraordinary pain and confusion.

Eventually I was allowed home, and in a rare moment of unity my parents and I went for a McDonald's. It's hard to express quite how strange that night was. I can't remember it as a single narrative; writing has come in fits and starts as I've tried to piece it together.

I later wrote to Al to ask him how he remembered the day's events as my memories are so hazy. It seems that mine was not the only memory mercifully blurry about what has become known as 'that day', but he wrote back with the following recollection:

> It was a completely normal day . . . a chill in the air, and the hope of a short break with family dangling in front of us as Christmas approached. I'm pretty confident that I saw you in the morning and it was a normal cheeky comment or two from me, and a rolling of the eyes from you . . . you know . . . business as usual!
>
> After lunch I saw Rebecca who had popped in – she had seen what you were up to and came to me to get help. We brought you to the Holy Hut and I got the deputy head. We arranged for you to get help.
>
> I remember you were drowsy as anything . . . You were completely zoned out and I was feeling completely out of my depth . . . I remember the worry, concern and sheer shock at what I was a part of . . . not in a negative way, but more in a way that allowed me to ask tough questions of myself as a caring stakeholder in your world. Had I missed something? Was there something I could have done? Had I failed you? Could I have prevented this?
>
> I remember how proud of you I was when you first came back to school. You and I had an understanding about 'that day'. We could talk about it openly – and I could be honest with you. I was safe in the understanding that I wasn't going to be the one who 'fixed' you . . . but I could be someone that supported you through the process of getting the help that you needed.

What I can recall is the silence that fell like snow over our home. I don't think we knew what to say to one another. How do you talk about the fact that your only daughter has tried to take her own life? That evening, I rang Simon to tell him what I'd done.

There was a new, deeper note of concern in his voice. I wondered if he, too, was remembering the girl so full of hope giving her life to Jesus on that boiling July day three years before.

He arranged to come and see me, and the following day a card from him plopped on to our doormat. It bore some words from Psalm 40 that I clung to – a life raft in the midst of what felt like a tsunami of shame and hopelessness.

> I waited patiently for the LORD;
>> he turned to me and heard my cry.
> He lifted me out of the slimy pit,
>> out of the mud and mire;
> he set my feet on a rock
>> and gave me a firm place to stand.
> He put a new song in my mouth,
>> a hymn of praise to our God.

I wasn't sure that I believed a new song would come from my lips, and I wasn't sure that I believed I'd be lifted from my pit, but I hoped against hope that the cries I kept silent would be heard.

The following day, much to everyone's shock, I went back to school. It was like returning to a crime scene and I spent most of the day in Al's office. Like Simon, he was trying to work out how it had happened. He'd been mere metres away from me, yet I hadn't spoken to him, and I'd done something that might have been irreparable. I apologized again and again, unable to see past my own disgust to his concern and Rebecca's. If anything, the overdose made me hate myself even more. It was the ultimate reason why I should die and somehow that was the thing that stuck in my mind. Not that people loved me, or that they wanted the best for me – it was that I'd done an awful thing and deserved to die.

During the days that followed, pills and razors were squirrelled away from me in an attempt to keep me from harming myself. It's something that happens all over the country as parents desperately try to keep their children safe. It's an understandable precaution, but it left me in a tailspin. The one thing I could do to keep control had gone – and with no possibility of injuring myself I searched for a new way to quell my self-destructive urges. I began to binge and purge.

In retrospect, I'd probably been bingeing for a while, stuffing my anxiety and disgust down by filling myself as fast as possible with food, but I began to do it intentionally, eating until I was uncomfortable and finding solace in emptying myself out, with my knees on the bathroom floor. The raw ache of my throat after each purge, the exhaustion, the tears that sickness would force from my eyes, became addictive. If I couldn't bleed it was the only way I could imagine of getting any relief from the chaos in my mind. It's important to remember, bulimia is as much self-harm as cutting. Writer Marya Hornbacher points this out, highlighting the violence of eating disorders: 'We think of bulimia and anorexia as either a bizarre psychosis or as a quirky little habit, a phase, or as a thing that women just do. We forget that it is a violent act, that it bespeaks a profound level of anger toward and fear of the self.'[2]

If anything, the overdose had cemented in my mind that I wanted to die. I was exhausted with life and dreading the upcoming appointment with the Child and Family Consultation Service that was scheduled for December. The letter announcing it signalled a hope that I would get the help I so desperately needed, but for me it also signalled fear.

The CFCS, as it was known to its clients, was tucked behind another school, in a building that looked as though it had been added as a hasty afterthought. Mum and I approached the door and pressed the bell, which was declared by a peeling sign to be for 'Mental Health'. As we entered I remember reeling in disgust at the place. There was a dirty brown carpet scattered with brightly coloured children's toys, and for some unknown reason the walls were covered in ceiling tiles. The lower tiles all looked like they'd been kicked to death, with gaping holes showing the equally chipped plaster beneath.

I gripped Mum's hand tighter as we sat down in the waiting room and within minutes, just when I thought nothing could be as bad as my first impressions of the place, I met Janet. To put it kindly, she was eccentric, but I honestly could have got over the horse teeth imprisoned behind dirty braces, the huge size 11 feet encased in pointed shoes, the ill-fitting skirt and the inane smile, if she hadn't also happened to be very bad at her job. As she led us into yet another battered room, Mum and I exchanged glances. It was like a bad sitcom.

The two of us sat in silence as Janet talked, her accusatory tone masked behind a smile that she never let slip as she asked me about the events leading up to the overdose. When she asked Mum to step outside, I recoiled, unable to believe that I was going to be left alone with this woman.

'So do you like risk?' was her opening gambit.

'Sorry?'

'I'm assuming you're into risky sports? Snowboarding? Abseiling?'

'Um, not really. I did it once at Centre Parcs. I don't like doing scary things.'

'Overdosing is risky.'

'I just wanted it to stop.'

'You wanted to stop engaging in risky behaviours?'

'I wanted to stop hurting.'

'So you didn't want to take risks any more.'

The conversation continued in a similar vein for a while as I convinced her that I was risk averse and 'just really tired'. It was a line I would use again and again with professionals over the following years.

Her notes from that meeting relay the following:

> Thank you for referring Rachel (sic) to the clinic. She was given an early appointment following a small overdose. I saw her with her parents and on her own. She looked pale and was often close to tears. It seems she took the tablets in a symbolic attempt to alleviate emotional pain and not as an attempt to die.

I returned to the clinic a week later and met my counsellor for the first time. As we went into the small, battered room, my eyes were drawn to the photographs of seascapes on the walls and, as I spoke about the most horrible parts of my life, I focused on the scenes that showed me the beauty of God's hand. Eve was a petite woman with smooth mahogany skin and kind brown eyes; she spoke softly, and during the hours I spent with her over the following weeks she listened patiently as I tried to talk about what I was going through. In truth, though, I didn't know how to open up properly; she was a stranger and I didn't understand what I was feeling, let alone how to express it. The only people I was 100 per cent honest with at the time, the only ones I felt able to tell how desperate I was feeling, were Al and Simon, who'd seen me at my glazed-over worst.

A few weeks later, at the annual Christmas ball that I attended with some friends, I set a smile firmly upon my face, ready to at least try and have a good time. Jessie was up from Devon and we had a lovely Christmassy afternoon before the ball, doing our make-up, watching *Love Actually* and excitedly making plans for that summer's school music tour to Italy that Jessie would return from Devon to be a part of, which was going to be the best trip I'd ever been on.

The morning after the ball, all the good fun of the evening before was wiped away in an instant. Once Jessie had left to go to a friend's house, Mum called me into her bedroom. She was pale and I could tell she had been crying. My stomach clenched and I wanted to escape, cut myself, purge or overdose. I didn't care. I couldn't face any more bad news.

Her voice shook as she told me that Elodie, a lovely lady from church who'd been baptized only months before and had a young daughter, had died of a heart attack. She had left behind a loving daughter and a doting husband – a life full of promise. The grief and anger that snowballed in my chest felt like it was burning my insides.

For the second time I disappeared into the distant space in my head. I wished it was me who had died. I had nothing to give. She'd had everything. If I could have swapped places with her I would have done, in the blink of an eye.

Christmas that year was not a happy one. The church reeled in grief at the news of Elodie's death, and the sermon Simon gave was on 'Love in a cold climate'. It spoke of God as Immanuel in the cold climate of grief and pain that we were experiencing. Elodie had said in her testimony, 'I still have questions, but somehow they seem less important. I know the trust I have in Jesus is stronger. I know now, you just need faith.' The poignant words of a woman who had died only three days before tore through me. They are words I've returned to time and again in recent years, and the sermon Simon delivered to us has resonated with me ever since, pointing to a hope that has grown with me:

> I believe there's help and inspiration for us here – in chapter 1 of John's Gospel. Its message tells us what God is like and how God can be known. It's a word that sounds as if it recognizes the pain in me – and the pain in you – in the real flesh-and-blood world of our lives . . . here's the gospel truth: 'The Word became flesh'. God has a human face in Jesus. God knows what it's like to be human.

I could barely hear the words through my tears, but I did know, perhaps for the first time, that God was present in the midst of my pain. I'd been asking where God was when it hurt ever since my first experience of bereavement at the age of ten. As Simon delivered his sermon to a broken and grieving church, I glimpsed something of God that I'd never seen before. This was a God who sent his own Son to leave the complete joy and majesty of heaven and live a messy human life. That Christmas morning I realized that, no matter how alone, no matter how misunderstood I felt, Jesus was, and would always be, present in the midst of it.

As 2007 began, those quiet realizations I'd found in my heart that Christmas Day had remained, but they'd once again been muddied by weeks of self-harm and bulimia. The urge to take another overdose was intensifying until it almost became an obsession, and every time I was in a shop I would hover in front of the painkillers, my hands itching to take as many tablets as possible to block out the deafening noise of my own thoughts and my violent self-hatred.

Back at school, I buried myself in work, drafting and redrafting my English coursework seven times until it met with my approval, working late into the night and guzzling coffee. The decrease in my food intake, coupled with a growing anxiety, meant that I spent most nights watching *Friends* re-runs until dawn before dragging myself to school.

Crisis was looming. I could feel it and the people around me knew it.

It happened at church one Sunday in the middle of January. There was the familiar 'snap' in my mind as I worked with Elodie's daughter in Sunday school. Convincing myself that it would have been far better if I had died in Elodie's place, I retreated into my head once more. By the time the church family lunch was served, it was obvious that I wasn't coping. Dad took me home via KFC. While he went to get our lunch, I took a detour to Superdrug, telling him I needed some new lip balm, and bought a packet of paracetamol.

That simple lie was a sign of how far I had retreated. My sense of morality was impaired and all I could see was the end, and how I could make it come as fast as possible.

I ate as fast as I could. I reasoned that I needn't bother about calories because I would, after all, be dead. In the back of my mind, it occurred to me that even if I survived, I could lose as much weight as I had done after the last overdose.

That thought set my decision into concrete.

Once alone in my bedroom, I thought no more of the after-effects of my actions. I wanted to die, and my path to death was clear. Popping the pills from their foil casing, I lined them up on my dresser. I swallowed them one by one and then sat on the corner of my bed, feeling nothing.

Slowly, I could feel myself returning to my body. I felt sick and clammy. Suddenly, death scared me. I tried to make myself sick, but my mouth was so dry it was totally impossible. My fear was becoming so great that I could see no option other than to go and face Dad to tell him what I'd done.

My entire body was visibly shaking – so much so that I made a conscious decision to retreat into my head. I remember nothing of my words to Dad except his shouts of 'Bloody hell' and driving like a maniac to church to get Mum.

The haunted, ashen look that hung on Mum's face still fills me with gut-wrenching guilt. Whipps Cross, the hospital I was born in and had stayed in so many times over the years, had never been my favourite place, but it took on a whole new role as the centre of my nightmares that day.

The nurse was brisk and brusque. She looked at me through disgusted eyes and we were made to feel like a total waste of her time. I was put into a side room in the emergency department and the nurse thrust a rough paper gown at me, leaving me to change into it. My parents returned and we sat in an uncomfortable silence. The agony in the room was tangible; it hung thick and dense.

Simon arrived, and for a while it seemed like the spell was broken. It was back to dealing with the present and making sure I would survive until tomorrow. When the doctor arrived, though, my first thought was, *He's far too hot for a situation like this*. Perhaps it was a sign that it was still me under the hospital gown?

Later on, I was wheeled down to the observation ward, Mum, Dad and Simon following, all of us taking part in a strange danse macabre.

Once we were seated on the ward, on plastic NHS chairs, our conversation was strangely mundane for such extraordinary circumstances. I said as much and we fell silent, the enormity of what was happening suddenly hitting each and every one of us. My ears were on high alert, every cry and mutter made my head spin. I was acutely aware of the man opposite me, growling to himself. The two security guards stationed either side of him exchanged furtive and knowing glances every few seconds.

Time came for Simon to leave. Mum said she should pop home to get me some clothes and other bits and pieces, while Dad would stay with me. I lost it then. I sobbed and cried with no thought of my appearance because I felt at that moment, as I had felt before, that my heart was cracking open in agony. It was as if my pain was permeating the atmosphere. I had been the girl who was going to go to Bible college and become a minister. But the girl who stood before him, eyes wild and wearing a paper hospital gown, the girl who lay among all those other people whose minds were bowing under the pressure of mental illness, had tried to end her own life. This was not how the story had been meant to pan out.

It was eventually decided that Dad would run home to get my things. Mum and I were left alone, suddenly unsure of what to do with ourselves now there were no distractions. Neither of us had the energy to face what was really happening, so we simply clung to each other.

With no warning, the muttering man opposite began to peel his clothes from his body. His voice rang through the humdrum of the ward, and the security guards pounced as his behaviour became steadily more erratic, expletives falling from his lips like acid rain. I grabbed my iPod and, trembling, I chose a recent talk of Simon's. I turned the volume up to maximum and his calming voice filled my ears. I closed my eyes as Mum clung to me and shut her eyes tightly against the distressing scene unfolding before us. Through the earphones, I listened to Simon's calm voice:

'But here's the gospel truth: "The Word became flesh". God has a human face in Jesus. God knows what it's like to be human. God is not indifferent! He does care. In fact, God couldn't care more – and so God did intervene. The light that was coming into the world stepped down into our darkness. God came to our rescue – to do for us what we couldn't do for ourselves – "the Man who is God" bringing us and God together – he came in love to be "God with us".'

And I heard in my mind the shortest of phrases:

'We've got to shine in here.'

I didn't know what it meant, or what effect it would have on my life; I hardly even understood the words. But I filed them away in my mind.

Shortly after the poorly fellow had been wrestled back into bed, Mum walked firmly and purposefully towards the nurses' station to request the empty private room, to save both of us the trauma of any further events. Our wish was granted and we hurriedly moved into the side room, both visibly relieved to be away from the rest of the ward.

Dad returned a while later and stayed until 11 p.m. I clearly remember watching *Wild at Heart* on the hospital television amid the busyness of the psychiatric ward. Till the day the series ended, I couldn't watch the programme again without being transported back to that place.

The following day, after a fitful night's sleep, I was shocked all over again to find myself in hospital, and shocked yet again when, once more, I remembered what I had done to myself and those I loved.

While I waited to see the child psychologist later in the day, my grandparents came to visit. We were frequently interrupted by an elderly Jane Doe, who seemed to like bursting into my room, as she had done so for the past 18 or so hours.

The child psychologist was, quite frankly, one of the most unpleasant, patronizing men I have ever had the misfortune to come across. He was rude and, being an 'expert' on 'teenage overdoses', had already made up his mind that I fitted exactly where I should on his spectrum. After a torturous hour I seemed to convince him that I wasn't about to take another overdose anytime soon, and he deigned to let me leave. We practically ran. Shoving my things into a bag haphazardly, we got out as fast as we could.

Once we were home, silence descended. I had a bath to clean the smell and feel of the hospital off my body and arranged to see Simon the next day. As I went to bed that night, the guilt pressed down on me in a whole new way, now that I had come back to the 'real world'.

The next day is a blur. I remember very little of it. Talking to Simon, facing the pain I had caused, I admitted that this time the aim hadn't just been to kill the pain, but to kill myself.

At an emergency appointment with another psychiatrist at the Child and Adolescent Mental Health Service, I once again pulled off a skilled performance, convincing the doctor that I didn't want to hurt myself and that I'd never wanted to die. Although I felt as though I'd managed to pull the wool over their eyes, I decided that I would never take another overdose. I felt such intense guilt at what I'd put everyone through that I couldn't face doing it to them again.

I didn't go back to school straight away this time. The experience had been more traumatic, my family and I more deeply scarred. When I did return to school, the story was that I had been hospitalized after a severe asthma attack. That week I spent a lot of time first in Al's office and then in Ms H's, going over the hellish events of that day.

Everything went quiet for a few weeks while I desperately tried to keep a grip on reality. I was haunted by what I'd done, and although the experience had instilled in me a desire to get better, I was also painfully aware that I didn't know how to begin.

The snow fell thick and fast that February. Everything glowed white and it seemed that the snow had put a smile on everyone's faces. The morning we awoke to that beautiful whiteness was the day my parents and I were supposed to have a meeting with Ms H. To say I dreaded it is putting it very mildly.

When I found out that my place on the music tour to Italy with Jessie that I'd been so looking forward to was under threat because of my overdoses, it felt like I had been winded. The event on which I'd focused my 'wellness' was apparently out of my reach and I was overcome once more with the futility of it all. I arrived in a soggy, sobbing heap in Al's office, grief pressing down on me like a leaden blanket. I could hear the jubilant shouts of fun from the snow-covered school around me and I felt myself drifting into my head. I walked around school that day not really taking anything in.

As the weeks passed I dragged myself on to an even keel. If getting well was what it took to be allowed to go on the trip of a lifetime, then I was going to do it. I stopped cutting myself cold turkey, and kept my secret binges to a minimum. Sessions with my mental health nurse Eve seemed to be going well too. I was facing up to the damage that I had done to myself and the reasons I had resorted to such drastic measures. It became clear, though, during the occasional family therapy sessions I sat through, that my parents' marriage was beginning to crumble.

I went to therapy less often and, although I was still seeing Al and Simon regularly, I was working hard, revising as if my life depended on it and focusing on the summer. I hoped I'd not only be going to Italy but also to a summer school at the London School of Theology, where I wanted to go to university. It seemed like a good way of getting a better feel for the place.

Yet again, however, the higher I got, the more worried those around me were as, when I fell, it was blatantly obvious that I would fall hard and fast. And fall I did. I started cutting and bingeing, slipping back into the pattern with ease. I was crying in lessons again and as home life became more difficult, the more I punished myself with food and self-harm.

I began to buy my own blades, keeping them in a small pink dust bag in my bedside cabinet. The blades sat in the bag along with dressings and tissues so that I could keep it as secret as possible. I'd established a routine.

Every night, the lights would go down, I would put on a playlist and cut at my legs, desperate for the moment's release as the catalogue of cuts and scars began to build up. When I heard someone move towards the stairs, I would shove plasters on and feign sleep, swapping the Goo Goo Dolls for Harry Potter.

Eventually I would fall fitfully and restlessly asleep, only to wake up and start all over again.

My decline was secret this time. I spoke to my head of year and made it seem that, yes, I was struggling, but I was also keeping a tight rein on my emotions and working as hard as I could. I managed to convince everyone around me that I was well enough for the music tour and I was granted permission to go – on the proviso that I wouldn't 'do anything stupid'.

Sessions with Eve, my mental health nurse, came to a close, and she wrote in her closing letter: 'It was lovely to meet with Rachael and to find out how well she is doing. It appears there is currently no need to continue with any more sessions with this department and as our service only goes up to 17, I will need to be closing her file here.' I felt let down that I'd so easily been able to hide what was really going on, that I'd been able to deteriorate without staff really noticing.

By the end of that summer, settling back after the Italy trip and summer school at the London School of Theology, I sensed a shift at home. The mood was different, calmer somehow, and one evening at dinner my parents announced they were separating. I was more relieved than I could put into words. The lightening of the atmosphere since their decision had been marked, and part of me thought it would remain so. The conversation that followed was what I had expected. I would live with Mum in the house, it wasn't my fault, and the fact that they didn't love each other any more had no bearing on their love for me. And for the most part I believed them – except for the niggling doubt that my ill health had been the straw that broke the camel's back.

As Christmas breezed in, along with the lights and joie de vivre, I felt oddly disconnected from it all. I was unarguably in a much better mental state than I had been the previous Christmas, but memories of the year before hung over my mind like a shroud. I wanted to be able to forget, but I didn't feel I deserved to forget the pain I had been in and the pain I had caused others.

It was the first Christmas after Dad had left. He had moved into a small flat in Streatham, but I had only been there once to help him move in. I preferred to see him at the hotel. Mum and I were determined to make it a different sort of Christmas, to distract from the obvious differences and so, abandoning tradition, we went out for Christmas dinner, much to the consternation of my beloved grandpa.

The day came and went. It was OK as Christmases went, but for the first time I realized that I was grieving. Grieving for the family we no longer had and grieving for the dad I felt I had lost for good.

After Christmas was over I buried myself in schoolwork and the January exams, working through every free period and most weekends. Despite my exhaustion, the constant work stilled my head, at least for a little while. I was self-harming every day to keep my emotions under control, and my eating was sporadic. I got through the exams, feeling I could have done no more to secure the grades I wanted and they had gone surprisingly well. Now all I could do was wait for the results.

Shortly after Christmas, I was persuaded to visit the doctor once more. My secret decline had come out into the open as I struggled to get through each day.

I saw Dr T, and after she'd listened to me she scanned my notes listing the overdoses and the abrupt end of my treatment by the Child and Adolescent Mental Health Service. As I sat before her, she faxed a referral to the adult mental health team. Within a day I'd been given an appointment.

The voice I heard down the phone had a soft Scottish accent, reminiscent of that of one of my favourite teachers from primary school. When I met him later that day I found myself pouring out more than I'd told anyone in months. I told him about my merciless attempts to restrict my eating, the feelings of failure that I wasn't able to starve myself, the fact that I was cutting more frequently and more deeply.

After three years, I was finally diagnosed with clinical depression and prescribed antidepressants for the first time. They allowed me to concentrate better, but they also stopped me crying – which led me to self-harm more often as I desperately tried to exorcise some of the demons within.

I was seeing David, the psychiatric nurse I'd had first contact with, weekly. While I felt I was getting through each day and managing, I was desperate to do myself some damage. I didn't want to take another overdose and risk hospital, so I focused my attention on laxatives. The feeling of emptiness never lasted long, but it was enough to quieten my mind for an hour at a time.

The day after my friends found out about the laxatives, I found myself flanked by two of my closest friends, sitting before the head of sixth form. I remember feeling completely numb. Numb to my friends' worry and numb to the teacher's concern. I was told in no uncertain terms that laxative abuse could kill me. Although at that point in time I didn't know how to say so, I hoped it would.

The head of sixth form wrote to my mum to tell her what was going on, and I felt cornered and angry. I couldn't see that I was doing anything wrong, because as well as keeping my brain quiet, I also believed I was hastening the time when I would no longer be a worry to anyone. The people around me reminded me of the danger I was putting myself in, the long-term damage I might be doing to myself, but I didn't believe there would be a 'long term'. I couldn't envisage myself lasting beyond the year. In fact, as the year went on I became more and more certain that I would be dead by my eighteenth birthday.

At the same time, however, I was also making plans for life after school and had begun having driving lessons. It was strange, planning for a future I half wanted but was sure would never come to fruition.

In early March, I had my interview for a place at the London School of Theology. I was excited and apprehensive in equal measure, but I was also sure that it was where I was meant to be, despite the anxiety and homesickness I had experienced during the summer school.

The day of the interview was bright and sunny. I dressed carefully in my suit and set off with Mum beside me. We were seated in the foyer and I was chatting nervously, along with the rest of the candidates. The next thing we knew we were being whisked away to have lunch with the current students. As we waved our parents and partners off, I prayed with a new sense of urgency; the day had finally arrived. I was warmly greeted by some of the friends I had made during the summer school and I managed to relax a little, although my throat was constricting with nerves and I struggled to swallow.

Another wait ensued before my interview, and I sat chewing my thumb and making lighthearted conversation with the other interviewees. I don't remember much of what followed apart from a rather awkward discussion about my 'mental health issues' and the swell of pride I felt when I answered a question about the value C. S. Lewis's *The Problem of Pain*, saying it was best read in conjunction with his other work, *A Grief Observed*. This prompted smiles and I felt my confidence grow as the interview progressed. Above all, I knew that I was doing what I felt to be God's will.

At home that evening I replayed the interview in my mind, feeling secure in the knowledge that I had done everything I could. The next day loomed on the horizon, a D-Day of sorts. I would be receiving the results of my January exams and finding out whether or not I had been accepted on to the Theology BA course that commenced in September 2009.

After my first lesson I rushed down to Mrs B to receive my RE result, my heart hammering like a long-incarcerated prisoner. The result quite literally took my breath away.

Four black symbols.

One hundred per cent.

I yelped with shock and joy. I'd done it! Not only had I got an A grade, I hadn't dropped a single mark. The blood and sleep lost to the exams hadn't been in vain.

I'd been instructed by the registrar to ring in mid-morning to find out the result of my interview, so at 10.30 I shakily dialled the number from Mrs B's office. My friends surrounded me, anxious to hear what was going to unfold and no doubt wanting to ensure that I would be safe if the news wasn't what I hoped it would be. I was touched that they all stayed, waiting silently while I was put through. Putting down the phone I slowly turned and shouted, 'I did it! I'm actually going to LST!' I'd already decided to take a gap year before embarking on a degree in the vague hope that I might achieve some kind of recovery before heading off – but their acceptance gave me something solid to aim for.

I was hugged be my friends and scolded by the librarian who heard my shout, but I didn't care, and as I went to get my history result I was beaming. I didn't really care how I had done – nothing could bring me down from the cloud I was floating on. I'd got a B in history. I floated higher and higher; I couldn't remember feeling so happy since my baptism nearly five years before. I can barely remember the rest of the day, except for the joy that radiated from me and the pleasure and pride of my family that, just for once, I could allow myself to feel and appreciate in all its beauty. It was truly a golden day, and I was comforted that my hard work and dedication had paid off in the way I felt it hadn't during my GCSEs.

My place at LST was secured on the proviso that I would have a doctor's letter the following April to confirm that my mental health was stable enough to embark on the degree course; I finally had a clear, long-term objective to encourage me to get well and stay well. My dose of antidepressants was increased every time I had an appointment with the psychiatrist and I was seeing David every week, sometimes more than once a week, to get me through particularly difficult days.

By the middle of March I was getting stuck into revision for my impending exams, determined that I was going to do better than I had done at GCSE. As I worked long into the night, that determination was simultaneously my saviour and my destruction. I was working harder than I thought possible, falling into bed exhausted each night but rarely staying asleep for longer than a couple of hours. At one point I was doing schoolwork 16 hours a day, trying to be the best I could possibly be.

The strain, unsurprisingly, was beginning to show. The less I slept, the more my brain fizzed with adrenaline, and I lost weight rapidly as I reduced my calorie intake to keep up the thrills as the number on the scales dropped day by day. I could sense the worried glances my friends exchanged as I sat at lunch with only a bottle of water once again, but I ignored them, unable to even conceive of the fact that they cared whether I lived or died.

Study leave rolled around – a strange time when you can get up when you want and basically do what you want because there's nobody to watch over you. Tempting as this was, my secret goal of flooring everyone with shock when I emerged with three A grades kept my nose in the books. I shared my ambition with no one because, as much as I wanted it, I was also acutely aware that I simply wasn't clever enough, and it was a well-documented fact that I didn't perform well in exams. But that ambition, however impossible to achieve, was what kept me studying day and night.

The exams were as stressful as I expected. Before I stepped into the exam room I was gripped with intense panic, and I wanted nothing more than to run away. I forced myself in, however, and got through them.

The day after my last exam, I felt utterly empty. I had filled my head with work for so long, managing to block out my feelings so effectively, that once revision had exited stage left, terror at my situation and the pounding thoughts in my head came crashing over me. To manage the feelings, I did what I had done so many times before and lost myself in my work. I decided to start reading some of the theology books I'd purchased to study in my gap year and started to try and write an essay on my shiny new MacBook, feeling incredibly cool, like a proper student.

A few days after my last exam I met Dr G, a psychologist I had been on the waiting list to see for six months. A tall, slim man with brown hair and kind eyes, he spoke with a gentle south African accent, and I found it very easy to open up to him. He realized during that first meeting that I was probably in for the long haul. As he arranged to see me again a few weeks later, I felt that maybe he would be able to help. Doctors had been trying to find me a clinical psychologist since I was 14; they obviously thought it would help and I had nothing to lose.

That summer, I began a work experience placement at the small private school I would be working at for a year before going to LST. It was a lovely school, the children in their bright blue uniforms accompanied by the unmistakable smell of play dough and pencils. I loved being there, and I felt I was doing well as I assisted the teachers in the last frantic weeks of the school year.

Yet, as much as I enjoyed the school, I was fast sliding into what I would come to know as 'an episode'. During one appointment with the psychiatric nurse I spent the entire time sobbing uncontrollably, pleading with him to let me leave so I could end it all. I was split between this relatively well-functioning 18-year-old who could focus at work, and a mentally ill girl on the edge of death.

Work experience was a refuge. Nobody knew what I was going through and I was able to hide. At the end of the week I had two days off to attend my leavers' day celebrations and dinner dance. Leavers' day was a surreal occasion; after form photos, book returns and giving out presents and thank-you cards to teachers, we set off for church. By now I was crippled with nerves because I'd agreed to sing the Leona Lewis song 'Footprints in the Sand' at the service. I found it somewhat ironic that I would be performing my first solo at school on my last day there, and my nerves intensified after my friend Phil emotively played a Frank Sinatra number on his saxophone, leaving many people, including me, with a lump in their throats.

I was shaking violently as I got up to sing, but once I began, I lost myself in the song. I put all the pain and joy of the last seven years into my performance, and despite a slight hitch when the pianist changed key in the wrong place I sat down again feeling exhilarated. People whispered their congratulations and after the service some expressed their shock that I could sing, because in seven years they had never heard me sing solo. I smiled and thanked them, but I was overwhelmingly disappointed that there had been a mistake. I had so wanted it to be perfect.

The following Monday, after a long day at work trying to swallow my tiredness, I went to my appointment with David and grief, anticlimax and loss broke over me. It had been the day I planned to end it all. Leavers' day and the dinner dance had both provided prime opportunities to say my goodbyes and round off my life. I wanted to die so much I was unable to contain my frustration that I was scared of death as much as I sought it. I spent two hours with David, going backwards and forwards: he wanted me to live, I wanted to die. I was in so much distress that I felt utterly desolate, quite ready to walk out of the room and into the path of an oncoming car. I wanted more than anything to make sure it worked. I didn't want to end up paralysed or locked up in some secure psychiatric unit. For the first of what would be many times I actually felt mad.

David eventually called Mum in to the room and gently explained to her what a dangerous position I was in. In his gentle way he told her that I was a danger to myself and wanted to die. He said he wanted to see me every day that week. She nodded mutely and I could see her trying to hold back the tears.

Here I was, her only child, who had fought so hard to stay alive as a baby and a toddler, and now I wanted to die. I can't begin to imagine the agony it must have been for her to have to watch me self-destruct. Every time I found another method of torture for my body, I know the pain she felt was physical and sickening. But, trapped in my own private world of self-destruction, I could not and would not reach out to comfort her. I knew that if I let her in, I wouldn't be able to kill myself.

On the way home she voiced her thoughts. 'Was today the day you wanted to end it?'

I nodded, mute, and she turned to face me.

'I'm glad you decided to stay.'

I sank into the car seat and closed my eyes. I was so tired.

I'm still not sure how I managed to make it through the week, let alone hold it together at work. By Thursday David had a bed ready for me in the local psychiatric unit. I managed to talk him round again, but I broke down at work, desperately trying to sort myself out in the toilets.

At the end of the week I was supposed to be going away to Dorset with Mum. David was worried I would use the holiday as an opportunity to end it all, but stronger than my desire to die was the fact that I would do anything to protect my mum. Unknown to me, Simon had written a letter to David persuading him that I would be safe with my mum and so we went away, and in the tiny cottage we had rented for the week I felt like I could breathe. It was a phrase David kept using; I didn't understand it, but it was true. The old saying about fresh air 'doing the world of good' was true in my case too; it wasn't a healer, but sea air and the beauty of my surroundings allowed me to think clearly for a little while. I wrote a lot and when we returned a week later I felt, if no less suicidal, then calmer and more able to face the battle of everyday life.

Now I had made it a fortnight longer than expected, I decided to hold out until after my birthday, which was a week away. What about after that? Well, I couldn't think further than my eighteenth. If I gave up afterwards, at least I would have given everyone a last memory. I would be able to have everyone I loved in the same room and tell them how much I loved them, how I valued them and how proud I was to call them friends. It could be the perfect way to say goodbye.

However, when my eighteenth birthday dawned bright and sunny, I smiled – I had made it to 18 alive. Not unscathed, but alive, and I was filled with a will to live – something that I hadn't experienced for a long time. I was going to make it. I wanted to make it. It's strange how positive I felt that day. I can only describe it as pure, unadulterated joy. Mum gave me a stunning Swarovski crystal jewellery set. It meant the world – it wasn't about the jewellery, though I adored it; it signified that everything she had given me was always her best, and I vowed that I would live, because I was loved in a way so many others aren't, and it would be an insult to my mum if I took my life and love away.

I went out for my annual birthday breakfast with my beloved grandpa. He had been taking me out on the weekend nearest my birthday since I was about eight years old, and it was a tradition I treasured. And as we ate our breakfasts – fry-up for him, crêpes with lemon and sugar for me – I enjoyed it just as much that year as I had for the last decade.

In the evening I had a party in a suite at my dad's hotel. I had invited everyone who meant the world to me, everyone I loved. I spent the evening in a happy champagne-filled haze, laughing, dancing, drinking and chatting with friends. Jessie and I stayed at the hotel that night and after midnight snacks from room service, the evening ended with Jessie passing out and me reacquainting myself with my first glass of champagne. Even this couldn't mar the night. It was practically perfect in every way and I was on top of the world.

By Monday, I had well and truly crashed back down to earth with an almighty bump. I felt as though I had nothing to look forward to except more people leaving my life. The hope and will to live I'd possessed in such abundance only two days before had deserted me and I sat in David's office in a catatonic state of grief. I couldn't focus on what he was saying; images of smooth, sharp, shiny razors flashed through my mind. I shook my head trying to get them out. David looked a little helpless as I repeated again and again that I wanted to die.

No, I don't want the crisis team.

No, I don't want to go into hospital.

Yes, I want to die.

No, I don't feel safe.

He watched me leave, looking sad, his care piercing through my agony. I got into Mum's car, leant back into my seat and closed my eyes.

'This is too hard,' I said.

Mum sighed.

All over again I would feel the agony and she would watch, helpless, as I flailed in desperation, hanging between life and death.

I saw Dr G the following day and heard in his voice too that he cared and wanted to help me get well. The following weeks passed in a blur. I don't remember much, except that David disappeared. One day he was there, making appointments with me every day, and the next he had gone on leave and nobody knew when he would be back. I felt completely and utterly alone. Dr G too was on leave for three weeks; Simon was on holiday. Mum was there, however, and as I tried to learn to lean on her, to tell her when I felt near the edge, we grew even closer.

I was also able to seek God. I began pouring my heart out on to paper, and as I wrote countless, sometimes illegible and unintelligible prayers I felt the burden lighten, ever so slightly. It was the first time that year I had opened up in prayer, a year-long struggle during which I'd sought self-destruction rather than God. I found that I could manage on my own, because I had a God who wasn't going to go on holiday or go AWOL or die. I learned to pray that summer in the only way I knew how. I wrote thousands of words of prayers, things that I would never have been able to articulate vocally, but which I could manage to lay before God on paper.

It was during that time that I first began to appreciate the importance of rest and routine for good mental health. It wasn't something I would get a grip on until many years later, but I did recognize its role in anything resembling recovery. It was during that time, too, that I was drawn to the story of Elijah in the Bible. For so long I'd convinced myself that even thinking of suicide would condemn me to hell. When I first read the story of Elijah fleeing to Horeb after Jezebel made him a marked man, I saw something of my own story reflected in the narrative.

Elijah was exhausted and, quite literally, running for his life. It's a strange contradiction that often appears in depression – running for your life and begging for death. Life is too terrifying to live, but death is still feared. The thing I found so encouraging about the story was that Elijah is a biblical hero – he's the guy who gets to stand beside the transfigured Christ in the promised land, who is whisked up to heaven – and yet here he is, burnt out and despairing. His struggles don't exclude him from working for God and God doesn't reject him in his distress. In fact, he draws close to Elijah by sending an angel to provide him with a rhythm of food and rest, something my family had provided for me during those darkest of weeks. There is also no condemnation as the angel responds to Elijah in the gentlest of ways, acknowledging what he's been through, saying, 'The journey is too much for you.'

The words leapt from the page. I felt as though I wasn't weak for struggling, I was human, and this didn't have to be the end of my story. At the time I didn't appreciate the tools that the angel gave Elijah for the next stage of his journey; regular sleep and food would doubtless have improved my mental health, but I was blind to the idea of self-care.

As August strolled towards its close, I began to gear up for my first full-time job. I was still slightly unsure about what my role would be, but the lure of the long public school holidays and eight-till-four days put my mind at ease. After all, even if I hated it, there were long breaks and I was only staying for a year.

As it turned out, I loved it. During the first few days I made friends with the principal's granddaughter, down to help her granny before heading back for her final year at Oxford. My boss, the woman with whom I would be sharing an office eight hours a day, began our working relationship in the following way. She shut the temperamental office door behind her and peered at me over her glasses.

'OK, there are a few things I want to tell you before we start. First, my bark is worse than my bite and, second, I do not suffer fools gladly, but you don't seem to be a fool so we should be fine!'

I smiled. I was going to like her, I knew it.

Lynne soon became known as my 'work mummy'. When, a few weeks into the term, I had to divulge my 'mental health condition', she was incredibly understanding and kind. We bounced off one another; sarcasm was our humour of choice, and we had great fun with it. Sarcasm may be the lowest form of wit, but I'm a firm believer that it's the funniest!

I enjoyed the work, and I enjoyed having a salary for the first time. The problem was that, in order to keep a tight rein on my emotions, I was tightening the restrictions around food more and more. It has been proven that a diet that contains little or no fat, even with a normal number of calories (which, of course, 800 a day is not), can induce and worsen depression. Given that I drastically reduced my food intake just as I was slipping into a dip, it was unsurprising that what might have been a blip turned into free fall. I was heading towards the abyss so fast my feet barely touched the ground.

It's often the case with a descent into depression that those around you are acutely aware you are losing your grip on sanity, but you cannot and will not see that you are simply not coping. It was a running joke at first, the box of Special K and the packets of Jaffa cakes I kept in my desk, all washed down with mug after mug of black coffee in an effort to avoid fainting. I went for walks at lunchtime to skip the awkward questions about why I wasn't eating, and tried to keep up a semblance of normality. In my mind at least, work was going well, so who cared if I fell apart as soon as I got on the bus? As long as I could keep up appearances I didn't care how deep I cut or how many diet pills I was taking.

At the beginning of the year I had signed myself up to attend an Overcoming Self-harm conference. I'd read the leader's autobiography the year before and felt this was someone who understood the maelstrom of emotions that accompany self-harm and its seductiveness. It was a weekend residential, and as it approached I began to feel increasingly nervous. It was uncharted territory on every level; I found it impossible to speak about self-harm to those closest to me, let alone to a group of strangers who would be able to see straight through the half-truths and diversionary tactics I had developed over the years.

By Friday evening, once I was packed and our departure was imminent, I began to have serious doubts. All of a sudden it was precisely the last place I wanted to be. With my second driving test coming up, at that moment all I wanted was to be able to practise my driving.

Despite my reservations, I still had a core hope that God would speak to me over the weekend. Mum reassured me that if it was unbearable, she was only half an hour away and could come and get me And so I made up my mind to go – clinging to the promise that I could be out of there within an hour if I so decided.

Through the wonders of Facebook, I had been in contact with a couple of other girls who were going on the weekend. After exchanging mobile numbers with a nice-sounding girl from Devon, and some rather frenzied texting, there was a knock on the door of my chalet, where Mum was helping me to settle in. Harriet bounced into the room with a wide smile and (my litmus test) sweet, smiling eyes. We chatted easily and I began to relax. After a while – once she had ascertained that I wasn't about to fall apart – Mum gave me a long hug, my hope and desperation sinking into the warm embrace I knew so well, and then she left.

Harriet and I went our separate ways briefly before dinner, and I sat on the single bed and read the card in the folder each of us had received. A group of women had been given our names and prayed for us before the weekend, and the message in round, curly letters sent a wash of reassurance through my exhausted, anxious body. It said that, during a time of prayer, the letter writer, despite never having met me, had felt I was very nervous and was being told to relax. Sometimes I'm a little dubious when someone says, 'God told me this . . .', but it was so sensitively done, it was exactly what I needed to hear. I felt uplifted and there was a spark of something that I hadn't felt for a long time. I think it was hope.

Shocked doesn't begin to describe how I felt when I walked into the main conference room and saw a girl with whom I had sung a few duets in youth services. I knew her well, if not personally. It was awkward for the first few minutes, but I was ultimately grateful for a familiar face and she was ready with a hug when I needed it most.

The first session focused on 'Hopes and Expectations'. I secretly hoped that I would experience one of those 'lightning flash' healings and all would be well. I didn't expect anything to change, but I wanted things to change very much.

On Saturday evening during the prayer time after the session everyone felt touched by heaven's light. As the song stopped, Abbie, the conference leader, stood and said she had a word for someone from Exodus:

'The Lord will fight for you; you need only to be still.'

I really did not want to go up to the front for prayer. It was something we had discussed at dinner that night: how we hated crying in public and how incredibly embarrassing we found going up for prayer. Yet the friend who had given me a copy of Abbie's book had written in it the very same verse. It was all too much of a coincidence for me. I stood shakily and walked to the front.

As I talked and prayed with Abbie I began to yawn uncontrollably, and as a lullaby was sung, I felt God speak in a very real way. It actually made sense. I couldn't fight on my own – I was too tired. I needed to rest in him and use his strength. I needed to relax into my heavenly Father's arms and let him take my burden. I collapsed into bed that night, still yawning, and felt a smile bloom across my face. I didn't know how and I didn't know when, but I knew that God would provide the rest I so desperately craved.

The New Year began, and things began to unravel. Again. Everything was suddenly a horrendous struggle; from getting on the bus to work each morning to answering the phone. It was all too much. I began having panic attacks, sometimes twice a day. I knew I was scaring Lynne. I was self-harming and not eating. Eventually I started to cry, and I knew then it was all over. I was just subsisting; I knew my standard of work had dipped dramatically and I also knew there was only so long I'd be able to keep up an appearance of sanity.

Dr G yet again voiced the idea of involving a crisis team who would visit my home and, if deemed necessary, arrange an inpatient bed for me. As I had done countless times with David, I refused. It simply wasn't something I could even bring myself to contemplate. I was numb to the possibility of a future. My mind couldn't settle and I sat in sessions with Dr G withdrawn, agitated and distressed. I thought suicide would be the only way out of a life that I couldn't conceive would ever get better.

I was sent home from work on the Tuesday afternoon after having panic attacks all day. Mum drove me home in silence – we knew, I think, that I had entered a new phase. Up until this point I'd always managed to keep attending school, and subsequently work. In the last two years it had become a refuge where I could bury myself in activity and ignore the violent storms raging within my soul.

Simon came over that afternoon and I was trembling with pain and agitation. I wanted to die. No afterthoughts or final revelations of the gift of life – I wanted to die and escape from the memories, escape from the intense self-hatred and run into death's welcoming arms. In death, I would at last be able to sleep.

Over the days that followed I slipped easily into the routine of illness. Left alone, with Grandma, Mum and Simon coming and going, I could have slipped into madness with very little effort. However, Mum was determined that as far as possible I would keep hold of normality. I wrote a lot and compiled a scrapbook of some of the lovely cards that had been languishing in a drawer, decorating it with quotes and pictures I had found. It was therapeutic being able to create something pretty and lovely rather than something steeped in depression's darkness and ugly shadows. I felt as if everything nice was fake, but I soon realized that smiles can come even in the midst of sadness. Happy memories can sit among present difficulties.

Sometimes all I needed was to be told a silly joke or to experience a random happening and for that moment I was 'back in the room', no longer trapped in my private hell. For while depression certainly hadn't been my choice, I did choose at times, due to my shattered self-esteem, to stay down. Languishing in the pit was certainly easier, and when you have no energy it's all you can do; however, as medication, rest and counsel begin to take effect, the choice becomes yours. To allow yourself to fall deeper, or to begin to claw your way out. It was my family and friends and a small dose of tough love that allowed me to begin my ascent towards the pinprick of light at the end of my tunnel.

During that time I read Pete Greig's book *God on Mute* and found that I related to much of what he wrote. I sought solace in the day before the greatest day – the idea that the darkest day comes before dawn. Holy Saturday was such a day, when all hope had died and no one knew that resurrection was just a sleep away.[3] As Bruce

Epperly describes it, 'Holy Saturday is the time in between death and resurrection, fear and hope, pain and comfort. Holy Saturday is the valley of grief and uncertainty, for us and for Jesus' disciples.'

It's the place where we spiritually live so often, when the worst has happened and we don't know if or how we can go on – yet in the midst of darkness we trust that dawn will break. It's often like this in the rest of life, I think. We often remember the most dramatic days, the happiest, but how often do we remember the days of silence, when everything is wrong but nothing can be done? I don't know if it's a good thing that we forget days like these in our own lives, but I think it would be good if we spent a little more time remembering Holy Saturday.

It goes beyond the agony of the cross, even. The day when it was finished – when Jesus was dead – because of our sins. It is a day of silence, it seems.

God doesn't always speak. Sometimes the silence of God says it all. As I write, I'm reminded of Job. Job who lost everything and everyone who mattered to him. Job whose friends were worse than useless. Job to whom God remained silent, waiting to speak. It strikes me that the silence of God is more often than not followed by a presence of God that is so awesome, so mighty, that we can do nothing but bow in praise and awe.

A season like this Holy Saturday can seem endless. It's the state in which we sometimes live our lives. It's an open wound. Shelly Rambo writes, 'The reality is that death has not ended; instead it persists. The experience of survival is one in which life, as it once was, cannot be retrieved. However the promise of life ahead cannot be envisioned.'[4]

There is no happy ending on Holy Saturday; the shadows of Jesus' death keep this day dark without a hope for the resurrection dawn. It's a mistake to rush beyond today, because it is reflected so often in life.

Holy Saturday continues the tradition of lament set out in the Old Testament, throughout the Psalms and, of course, Lamentations. It tells us that even when God is silent, he is still to be trusted. The desire for suicide is full of the same grief, despair and hopelessness that was present on that first Holy Saturday. The theology of Holy Saturday speaks to the pain and intense hopelessness that can reign in suicidality, and promises that, while life during such a period can seem hopeless, there is hope that Holy Saturday will end, beckoning in the defeat of death in resurrection. We can look forward to that day in the new creation when there will be no more pain. I hoped against hope that something new would start in me.

It's a theology that has been somewhat lost in contemporary, evangelical church culture. The phrase 'But Sunday is coming' is one I've heard a lot at Easter, though I believe it's important not to rush past the silent days of lament. We have to be able to deal with the times when God does seem to be on mute, to be absent, and the Psalms provide for us a pattern of lament and praise, doubt and faith.

I emerged again from the darkness and life continued quite steadily for a while, the shadows receding, allowing me to live a little. I did some normal teenage things – going to the pub, shopping – things lots of people my age were doing. Clubbing, however, was something my illness wouldn't allow; even the thought of it brought me out in a cold sweat and had been known to induce panic attacks. I wasn't going to ruin my steady mood by doing something I was uncomfortable with.

As the days began to warm up and the Easter holidays approached, I was looking forward to some relaxation and to catching up with old friends. It didn't happen like that. It was becoming abundantly clear that I was moving on a different plane from my school friends. We hadn't fallen out, but I found I had little to say to them, and I knew they felt the same. I didn't know how to explain what my day-to-day life was like, isolated as I was and hidden in mental illness.

When I felt my mood slipping slightly, I brushed it off as loneliness, and I was sure it would fade once I was back at work among the friends I had made there. Once the holidays were over, though, I began to make mistakes at work again. I wasn't sleeping and I knew I was heading for another fall, but at that stage I had no idea how steep it would be.

Two weeks into the new term, amid the mania of a school office in the final weeks of the school year, I was unravelling at a previously unheard-of rate. I felt sick with nerves every morning before work, petrified that I would make mistakes; and every time I did make a mistake – however small – I would have to go into the toilet and pinch myself to keep my head from floating away into the ether.

I started crying again and it was all over. I tried desperately to keep it together, but by Thursday it was crystal clear that I couldn't go on. Lynne told me repeatedly to go home; every time someone entered the office they commented on how ill I looked. This did nothing to help my self-esteem, which by that point was totally non-existent.

I didn't go in on Friday. I stayed in bed, unable to muster the strength of will required even to wash or to change my clothes. At two o'clock Simon appeared on my doorstep and I stood in front of him, my body quivering with sobs that I couldn't release. He sat with me and I asked him to talk about something inconsequential, something that might bring a smile to my face. And so he told me lots of wonderfully useless information about his football team, Crystal Palace, trying to bring something resembling a smile to my pale, exhausted face. When he left, I collapsed back into bed and sleep rolled over me in waves. Finally, I thought.

Rest.

The following weeks, yet again, are a blur. I don't remember them for the most part because I was trying very hard to die. I was at the end of my tether with life and I wanted to find the quickest way out. I was vaguely aware of the worried exchanges taking place around me, but I had so little concentration, or will to concentrate, that I couldn't take into my head anything that was being said, let alone allow any of it near my heart.

I made a failed attempt to return to work and was sent home at lunchtime feeling utterly wretched at falling apart again. On visiting the doctor's the next day I was signed off for the week just gone and the one that was to follow. I was relieved. I would be able to hide and not have to concentrate on anything other than my desire to die.

Simon recalls me being unreachable; I spent my time curled into a foetal position, talking about the abyss that I felt I was staring into, unable to see hope or a future, alternating between silence and tears. He felt I was slipping away from life, lost to the world behind my blank stare. He told me later that at times he would leave drained, unable to do anything but sit in his parked car and cry. Yet even at those times he believed in me and refused to accept that my story would end in darkness. He and my mum hoped on my behalf until I could hold my own hope.

On the Monday, I had a CPA – Care Plan Assessment – review. It's a risk assessment, a medication review and a therapy review. Simon accompanied me, as I have a habit of not remembering what's been said at these meetings and Mum was growing increasingly impatient at the lack of information I was giving her.

It was somewhat surreal. Here were Simon and Dr G, the two men who knew more about me than anyone else, sitting in the same room, talking about me. As they talked both to me and about me, I felt we were all aiming for the same goal: first and foremost, to keep me alive, and second to get me to LST. It was these two goals that I believed would give me the best shot at life. I had a sense that if I could just get to LST, I might find the hope I so desperately needed. I was searingly honest about the diet pills, my diet and the all-consuming desire to die. The meeting showed me a glimmer of hope and I was determined to make the most of it.

Although the seed of hope was embedded deep within me, I allowed myself to slip back into the abyss. It had become a comfortable place for me. I knew it was dangerous to stay there, but I honestly felt that I had little choice. At the same time, though, the final term at work was manically busy and I was enjoying it. At work I had found a place where I felt that I fitted. For the most part, the eight hours I spent there each day enabled me to push aside my pain and pretend I was a normal 19-year-old. I had never felt as though I belonged anywhere except church before, and as the time approached to say goodbye, I felt that, despite the hellish periods of depression, I was leaving somewhere I had been happy.

My last day at work was lovely. It was as frantic as ever and the familiar buzz filled me. At lunchtime, it was time to officially say goodbye. I was presented with a lovely necklace and lots of book tokens. I smiled – how well they knew me! When I returned to my desk there was a Tatty Teddy from Lynne waiting for me, with a large thank-you card. As I opened the card, which everyone had signed, I felt a lump rise in my throat; it was filled with kind goodbyes, thanks and declarations of how much I would be missed. I smiled and wiped my tears away; despite the agonies of the year just passed, I knew my memories would be fond ones.

I felt like a character on a TV show as I filled a huge cardboard box with my belongings and cards. Bidding farewell to Lynne was undoubtedly the hardest; she embraced me and smiled. She alone of everyone at work knew the depths of my struggle. As the tears started to fall in earnest, she admonished me and sent me off with a final hug for my leaving drinks.

I hoped against hope that LST would be a place where I could learn to live, but I wasn't sure I even knew how to live any more. The future seemed impossibly daunting.

4 Resuscitation

Before I knew it, September had arrived, and with it the beginning of my degree course at LST. I passed my driving test at the seventh attempt and packed up my belongings, ready to venture into the unknown. I was by no means well when I left, but I'd made a decision a few days before I went that I was going to be myself. If no one liked me, that was what I expected. And if they did – I'd have to find a new way of living.

I set off to Northwood, driving on a motorway for the very first time, my car filled to the brim with my belongings, and Mum behind me in her car, filled with my books.

It wasn't the easiest of starts. Panic engulfed me as it had done so many times before, and I cried for much of the first few days, desperately homesick and unable to work out how I was going to live in this new world with people all around. It was hard to hide, of course, with mascara streaming down my face and my hands shaking almost constantly. The people I met embraced me, however; notes were delivered under my door to encourage me, and even I found it hard to shrug off such acts of kindness as something they just 'had to do'.

On the first evening I went to an event called 'Committee on the Couch', which introduced us freshers to our student committee. On the sofa sat a slim olive-skinned girl with dark brown eyes; when she introduced herself I knew I wanted to be her friend.

'Hi, my name is Kelly and I'm from Essex and I'm the entertainment secretary. I can't swim and I'm a bit asthmatic.'

I smiled as I thought, 'Me too!' When I went up to speak to her at the end of the evening, she gave me a hug and her number, saying we should meet for coffee, almost as if she sensed I was struggling. Bolstered, I joined the others at the local pub.

By the time the first chapel service came around a few days later, however, I wanted to give up. I was terrified of this new life and of studying for a degree. As we sang the familiar worship songs I felt as though I were a fraud and there was no way I would be able to complete a degree or stay away from home – I just couldn't do it. So I got behind the wheel of the car and drove as fast as I dared down the M25.

Nearing my house, I pulled over at a nearby estate, wondering how on earth I was going to explain to Mum that after all the fight to get me to LST I was giving in. I phoned her from my car, just a few hundred yards away from my house, knowing it wouldn't be an easy conversation.

I don't think I'd ever heard Mum quite so angry as she was on the phone that day when I called her at work. She was less concerned that I'd left college and more so that I'd told no one and, while in such a state, driven on a motorway for only the second time. She phoned Dad and for the first time I could remember, he dropped everything and came running. I spent the afternoon on the sofa alternating between sleeping and crying as he sat and rubbed my back.

When Mum returned from work she hugged me as I cried again and together we spoke to the principal. He was encouraging and kind, assuring me that they wanted me to be a part of their community, but I wasn't a prisoner there and could visit home as often as I wanted. At the end of the phone call I decided to go back the next morning after a good night's sleep.

I was welcomed back with open arms the following day. My new-found friends said how much they'd missed me and how glad they were I was back. As soon as I started my lectures the following day I knew that I'd made the right decision.

As term progressed, with essays to write, countless books to read, and lots of colour-coded notes, I was loving it. It was amazing to be studying for a degree, and to be learning more about God as I did so. I was amazed, too, particularly considering the rather rocky first week, how settled I felt; yes, there were days when I wanted my own bed and a cuddle with Mum, but I felt at home at LST, blessed with the freedom I had to learn about the Bible and the Church, and how to use what I was learning to carry out God's calling in my life.

I was so challenged by the people and the teaching to live my life without relying on earthly things and people, which can so easily fall away. We spent our Old Testament Survey lectures focusing on the story of Abraham – on the promises God made him and the actions Abraham had to take. Called as he had been to leave his home, family and everything he was familiar with, I felt a little affinity with him in the first few weeks – and I'd only moved a 40-minute car journey away! God used Abraham in a mighty way, but I am sure there were times when Abraham wondered when, if ever, the spectacular promises God made him would come to fruition. And yet Abraham held on, slipping a little on the way, but clinging to the covenant God had made with him.

There are a multitude of lessons to be learned from how God used Abraham, and from how Abraham leant on the promises and trusted God when everything was against him. I was learning to learn to live more fully, love more deeply and trust more surely.

I could feel myself changing over the course of the days that passed. The decision I'd made to be myself meant I was making friends fast and, despite my self-hatred, people seemed to like me. Even though I'd cried my way through the first week and run away on day three, I made true friends and felt, for the first time, something close to popular.

It was a strange time. I loved my life, but I still hated myself, and I didn't know how I could manage to hold the two opposites together. When someone noticed a recent cut, though, I didn't see anything like judgement in his eyes.

'I burned it with my straighteners,' I said, looking directly at Luke, a second year I'd spoken to a few times before.

'Rubbish, but it's OK. You can come and talk to me if you ever get down.'

Nothing more was said about it, but he would become one of my closest friends. Reactions like his were common that first term at LST and I found to my surprise a love and acceptance that I'd never allowed myself to experience before.

I felt as though I was learning a whole new way of living; and I loved studying a course that helped me learn more and more about God. I received lots of prayer for healing, and in late November I had an encounter with God that I will never forget.

I was being prayed for by a member of the student committee and he told me that he felt there was something I needed to let go of.

I knew immediately what it was. While I'd been making strides in my mood and was self-harming far less, I'd been restricting my eating so much that the pounds were falling off me. I'd even fainted a few times. Most people had noticed that I rarely ate normally, with my Special K and bowlfuls of spinach as everyone else tucked into roast dinners or pasta.

'If I'm going to be free, I think I need to let myself eat more.'

I whispered the words so quietly that no one could hear me. I began to cry, and while there was no immediate feeling of freedom I decided to put myself to the test straight away. Slipping out, I headed to the vending machine and selected a KitKat; shaking, I unwrapped it and ate it slowly, savouring the crunch and the rich creamy taste. It was the first chocolate bar I'd eaten in a year and I felt triumphant.

It wasn't the end of my eating disorder, but it marked a change. It was the first in a series of decisions that committed me to life rather than death. I was starting to choose life. As my first term ended, I wrote an email to Al and Simon to try and articulate some of the things that had happened to me over those weeks.

> I have only been at LST for a few months and yet it feels like home. In those months, I ran away, smoked a few cigarettes, harmed myself, starved myself further than ever before . . . then looked at myself, looked at God, and realized that girl cannot serve two masters, girl cannot serve food and God, girl cannot serve her own strange default to self-destruction and the God she has professed to follow all of her days. So I chose to only serve God, and I make that choice all over again every single day.
>
> If you had told me I could eat a bag of chips and not want to throw it up I would not have, could not have, believed you.

If you had told me I would have eaten my first sausage in two years, that I would be eating very nearly healthily, normally – I could not have believed you.

And yet, this is the amazing thing about it – I am the girl who weighed herself 12 times a day, ate nothing more than cereal and soup, clung to her illness/disorder/self-destruction, actively sought new ways to hurt herself. I am also the girl who not so long ago decided to let go. I am the girl who is starting to live. More so, I want to live. I want to continue studying in this amazing place with these amazing people. I will not let myself fall back into the depths of hell.

I am all these things, but you know what I have realized, possibly for the first time in my living memory? I am a child and creation of God. That I have worth because I was created by him and it was never my place to destroy the body he created and gave to me just because it was hurt by someone else.

I almost sound flippant. I do not mean to. I am aware that I have a really long way to go. There are still thoughts in my head that I neither want nor deserve. I cannot forget what happened to me and what I did to myself, but I can start. I have made this commitment to life, to come to terms with these things in me and in my past. I have bad days and sad days, days when I fear I am slipping back into those depths I know so well, but beneath it, there is the hope of heaven that for so long I could neither see nor believe.

After so many years of being unable even to envision what life could be like, it was a huge turnaround, and it had happened relatively quickly. For the first time in five years, I felt as though I was really living. The words from Joel 2.25–27 I'd been given before I started at LST seemed so apt:

I will repay you for the years the locusts have eaten –
 the great locust and the young locust,
 the other locusts and the locust swarm –
my great army that I sent among you.
You will have plenty to eat, until you are full,
 and you will praise the name of the LORD your God,
 who has worked wonders for you;
never again will my people be shamed.
Then you will know that I am in Israel,
 that I am the LORD your God,
 and that there is no other;
never again will my people be shamed.

There was a freedom I couldn't remember feeling for many years; but I didn't always choose to use that freedom in the most productive of ways. I took up smoking and drank more than my fair share of wine during those months. They felt like my own private long-awaited rebellion (not that anyone really knew about the smoking – it was a secret, and thus not particularly rebellious), and I hadn't yet grasped that my body was anything that should or could be valued. I felt like Bambi learning to walk; getting stuff wrong and tripping over myself as I tried to live the years I'd lost.

It was undoubtedly a strange time. I was still self-harming occasionally, still sometimes overwhelmed by grief and sadness. The difference was that I had hope there was going to be a future. And more than that, I wanted there to be a future. Hope made a world of difference – it made me want to look forward.

A few months into 2010 I began to arrange my summer placement. I'd told my supervisor that I thought I wanted to do something around mental health, and within a few weeks I had a meeting with two members of the spiritual care team at the local mental health trust. I'm pretty sure I saw the glory of God in the two women I met who worked in the chaplaincy service on a general mental health ward. There was something very beautiful about the work they were doing and the encouragement they gave me in enabling me to be a little part of that work as part of my degree. They recommended a book called *Mud and Stars*, and that strange juxtaposition between the dirt, darkness and ugliness of mud and the beautiful shining light of stars seemed to capture both the ugliness of mental illness, the pain it causes, and the beauty and creativity it can create.

I couldn't tell you what struck me so much about the idea of mud and stars, only that it seemed to speak to my growing hope that there would be something to show for the hell I'd been through – that it would have been for a reason, a purpose. The idea lingered throughout the rest of the year, and when I began my placement that summer it exploded in my heart and my mind.

It wasn't easy. The first time I stepped through the doors of the mental health unit I felt a wave of nausea so strong it nearly knocked me off my feet. The unique smell of body odour and stale cigarette smoke whisked me back through the years to one of the worst days of my life, and I didn't know if I would be able to cope. I was shaking as I walked round the ward. The pain and heartbreak of the place was palpable, almost as if everyone's stories had clung to the walls.

I spent much of my time on an acute unit, where more than anything it seemed that people just wanted to be able to tell their stories. I heard accounts of hallucinations and delusions, of starvation, and I recognized in many others the blank stare with which I myself had greeted the world.

I found it hard to see other women of my age, some of whom had been through countless wards, covered in scars and refusing food. Each day I felt as though I was seeing the other paths I could have travelled on and that, by the grace of God, I'd avoided. With every new person I met, the long-forgotten words circled in my mind:

'We've got to shine in here.'

If Jesus had spent his earthly life with the most forgotten of people, in the darkest of places, I felt sure that the Church had to shine more brightly in places like this, where hope was seemingly lost. My heart broke again for the people who'd spent not just one night on mental health wards, but years; for the people I'd spoken to whose doors remained open 24 hours a day, with nurses stationed outside to ensure their safety.

A few weeks after the end of my placement, I had a very strange experience. I went to bed as usual one night and within a few hours I jolted awake. So far, not so strange – in fact, typical of my erratic sleeping habits – but the words *Think Twice* seemed to have been imprinted on my brain. I couldn't think of anything else and so I wrote them on a scrap of paper at my bedside.

An hour later, I woke up again with the image of a butterfly. I scribbled it next to the name and went back to sleep.

The following morning I stared at the roughly drawn butterfly and the words.

This is going to be something, I thought.

I reshuffled the blog I'd begun when I started at LST and put together one dedicated to mental health, calling it ThinkTwice. I got a friend with Photoshop to design a logo. I started a Facebook page. All in honour of something that didn't yet exist, but I knew, in some way, would exist one day.

I had no idea what on earth it was going to be, but I felt that the paper in front of me held something significant, a way for me to bring something good from the agony. The redemption of my lost years became something of an obsession. I had to make something valuable come from the years I hadn't really lived.

I thought about the meaning of redemption, what it means to live a life of the redeemed. I wondered if, as we live the life of the redeemed under Christ, our past and memories can also be redeemed.

Redemption is a vast biblical theme. God calls himself our Redeemer over two dozen times. The vocabulary of redemption appears around 150 times throughout the whole Bible.

In the Old Testament, redemption seems to have three distinct elements. First, the circumstance someone needs redemption from; second, the price to be paid for that redemption; and, third, a human intermediary acting to secure that redemption. In the New Testament we see Jesus acting both as payment and intermediary.

Jesus is our redemption.

He is both the instrument and the musician of redemption.

The melody of redemption is heard in his ultimate sacrifice. He died for us when we were still sinners – paid the price for our sin with his life.

It blows me away.

Psalm 103.1–5 says this:

Praise the LORD, my soul;
   all my inmost being, praise his holy name.

Praise the LORD, O my soul,
   and forget not all his benefits –
who forgives all your sins
   and heals all your diseases,
who redeems your life from the pit
   and crowns you with love and compassion,
who satisfies your desires with good things
   so that your youth is renewed like the eagle's.

God doesn't just give us back what we have lost – he gives us more than we could ever have imagined. When we think all is lost, he is waiting to give us more than we could ever find. He doesn't just lift us out of the pit – he crowns us. Crowns us with his love and his compassion.

So often in my life I have grieved hopelessly over what has been lost. I have felt lost in the pain of what has gone. And yet it's all too easy to forget how much God has already redeemed for us; he has redeemed our very lives so that we may one day be able to see him face to face.

Every stuff-up, every bad day, every painful memory, every heartbreak is redeemed by God through his Son. Which means that so much has already been redeemed. And there is so much more to come. It doesn't mean we don't have to face the pain, but it does mean he has something far greater, far more beautiful in store for us.

How can we fail to praise a redeemer who makes the putrid pure and the ruined the rescued?

As I fixed my sights very firmly on redemption, I couldn't help but begin to grieve for that from which I had hoped to be redeemed.

If my first year at university had given me a taste of what life could look like, my second year was a time to grieve for a life un-lived. Feeling unimaginably guilty about what I'd subjected my family and body to, I began to find it hard to look at the cross again, unable to comprehend how I could be saved when I felt like such a mess. Tears fell freely and I started having more panic attacks. I would appear at Luke or Kelly's door, eyes vacant, struggling for breath. Luke describes it as if I were in screensaver mode. At those moments I had no personality, just fear. The only way he could be present with me was to treat me as normal until I came round, as Kelly brought the faintest ghost of a smile to my blank face.

During one particularly awful panic attack, I bumped into one of my lecturers. As he led me, blinded by panic and tears, towards his office, we arrived at the office of Anna, my ethics tutor. Deciding that perhaps she would be better placed to help me in that moment, he steered me into her office, whispered to her and left.

Anna guided me to the chair in front of her desk and took her seat.

'Do you want to tell me about it?'

I burst into tears and cried for a long time. She came to crouch beside me, handing me tissues at regular intervals.

From then on, Anna and I met regularly. We prayed together, lamented together, raged together. We sat in silence and together 'We learnt to listen to the silences and to stand in solidarity with the silence of suffering in and through our friendships.'[1] I was allowed to be fully myself; there was no separation between dealing with Rachael and dealing with my mental illness.

Anna and my friends simply allowed me to be, and taught me that was more than enough.

They formed the circle of care that Simon had talked about so often. Between Luke and Kelly, Anna, my mum and Simon himself, I felt I could face my illness in a way that I hadn't been able to as a teenager – but I didn't know how to begin to approach God with the pain. I felt guilty for letting him down and being a burden to my friends. The circle of care came together to hold me when I was at my weakest and enabled me to come before God in a way I couldn't do alone.

The friendship I received was like that we see in the story of the paralysed man who was lowered through the roof to Jesus in Mark 2. These men were so desperate to bring their friend into contact with the healing power and presence of Jesus that in the heat of the Capernaum day they dug through someone's roof to beat the crowds and sit at Jesus' feet. It was an astonishing act of friendship; not least because I doubt the owner of the house was particularly enamoured with them in the aftermath. And while we probably won't have to dig through ceilings for our friends, by its very nature true friendship breaks down stigma.

John Swinton and Jean Vanier write in *Mental Health: Inclusive church resource*: 'The call of Jesus is to hear the cries for love and to move forwards in friendship and in perseverant love; a mode of friendship which destroys stigma and opens up space for all of us to be fully human even in the midst of our wildest storms.'[2] This is fierce friendship – it's not for the faint-hearted – but it was demonstrated to me by those who sat with me during those dark days and was modelled by Jesus during his earthly life. The way in which he offered friendship was radical; it focused not on someone's outward appearance, nor even on what Jesus may or may not have had in common with that person, but on the individual's own unique personhood. It reached across the social boundaries of the day, from the Samaritan woman in John 4.7 to Zacchaeus in Luke 19.2. As the Church, friendship is our greatest weapon against the stigma of mental illness, just as it was a weapon against the stigma of leprosy in Jesus' lifetime.

My friends offered me this friendship in a myriad of ways: praying with me, helping to ground me during panic attacks, forcing me to bed when I'd worked myself into a sleepless hysteria, and they wouldn't let me hide behind the pretence that this wasn't mental illness. They faced it and acknowledged it, which in turn allowed me to do the same.

So often within the Church, we shy away from caring for those in our midst who have mental health problems because we don't want to step on the professionals' toes. Offering friendship, however, is exactly the role of the Church, enabling people on the fringes of society to feel they are welcome and that they belong, regardless of what their lives look like. Sometimes we don't make it the safe place it is meant to be. The sanctuary, that safest and most holy of places, can instead feel intimidating. Rather than being made welcome, people can experience nothing beyond a handshake after the service.

Enabling our churches to become truly safe places extends way beyond making them physically accessible to making them emotionally accessible. To people at their weakest our songs might only proclaim victory and power, our sermons may make no reference to emotion. Even some of the most traditional aspects of our church services, such as the peace offering, can be terrifying for someone struggling with anxiety.

In these cases, it's not about abandoning our practices and donning sackcloth and ashes for every service, but about making space for those who may not be able to relate to God in the same way that we do. We want to enable people to come into our churches as they are and to be transformed by Jesus – not by church culture. It might be as simple as not asking everyone to sit at the front, or encouraging people that they don't need to pretend. Or it might be, as one of my friends did last Christmas, to hold a 'Blue Christmas' service of lament, allowing those for whom Christmas is a struggle space to lament before God, away from the cries of jubilation.

As seen in the oft-quoted passage from Ecclesiastes, there was a clear sense in our Jewish heritage that there is both a time for joy and a time for grief; and that message is one the Christian Church needs to reconnect with. Lament isn't a dirty word, nor is it less a form of praise than songs of jubilation; in fact, sometimes it's altogether more costly to proclaim God's sovereignty in the darkness than in the light. I can't help but think the art of lament is one that needs to be recaptured. It allows us time to process the Holy Saturdays of our lives before rushing into our Sundays of celebration.

There is a time to 'rage against the dying of the light' – the effects of the fall, the pain of this life and the distance between us and God. The beauty of lament is that it's more than complaint; it's an address to the Creator of heaven and earth. J. Todd Billings writes, 'Lamenting with the Psalmists is a practice that is counter to our consumer culture. Lament fixes our eyes on God's promises and brings the cries of confusion and pain – our own and those of others – before the covenant Lord.'[3]

Lament rages in the knowledge that what we experience on earth isn't the end of the story – it's merely a chapter in a greater story. It expresses our need for relief and deliverance, while also trusting that God can and will work in us and in our situation.

It was lament as the Jews cried out in their slavery in Egypt.

It was lament as Elijah cried to God from Mount Horeb.

It was lament as Jesus cried, 'My God, my God, why have you forsaken me?'

It is lament that invites God into our pain with the hope and expectation he will work in it.

The honesty in lament, for me, was one of the most important parts of recovery. Since I was 16, Al had told me that if I was able to be honest with God and those around me, mental illness would be easier to manage. As much as I hated to admit it, he was right.

The ability to be completely honest about how I was feeling, not only with others, but with myself and God, gave me a freedom I hadn't anticipated. Voicing my hopelessness has given me hope; and it's shown me a little of what sharing hope looks like.

As I entered the third and final year of my degree, I turned my attention to the subject of my dissertation. Years before, I'd seen a book called *A Psychology of Hope: A biblical response to tragedy and suicide* on the shelves of Foyles and decided that one day I would write something about suicide and the Bible; now I ordered the book and began work. I'd read Henri Nouwen's *The Wounded Healer* the previous year and had been captivated by the idea of using our own pain to help others. Using his book as a framework, my dissertation would look at how the Bible and the Church could offer hope and comfort to those struggling with thoughts of suicide.

The idea of a 10,000-word essay excited me, and I loved the idea of a wounded healer. Nouwen writes, 'For a deep understanding of his own pain makes it possible for him to convert his weakness into strength and to offer his own experience as a source of healing to those who are lost in the darkness of their own misunderstood sufferings.'⁴ His image struck a chord in me and helped me to process coming to terms with my past and discern more clearly my calling, which I was beginning to feel sure would involve talking about mental illness.

The more I looked at the idea of wounded healers, the more I was drawn to the account of Jesus' walk to Emmaus in Luke 24.13–35. Again and again I have been astounded that after all he'd gone through in the preceding days – the night of blood-soaked tears, the betrayal by his closest friends, the humiliating death, the day in the silence – Jesus spent his first morning listening to a couple of heartbroken friends.

Jesus, who could have healed their pain in an instant by revealing himself and his miraculous resurrection, instead walks with them, hears their pain. Psalm 107 says, 'Let the redeemed of the Lord tell their stories', and Jesus is doing just that. Even though he knows more about what has come to pass than they do, he wants to let Cleopas share with him.

After listening to Cleopas' story, Jesus tells his own. He walks Cleopas through everything the Scriptures say about him. I can imagine him taking Cleopas through Isaiah and the passages that talk about the suffering servant, recounting the words of the psalm he repeated on the cross: 'My God, my God, why have you forsaken me?'

What is clear is that Jesus' presence is captivating. The journey between Jerusalem and Emmaus is about seven miles, but they don't want it to end, so they invite Jesus in.

When Jesus breaks bread with these exhausted and hopeless travellers, everything changes. The intimacy of sharing a meal is what makes it so great for going out on a date, but it also makes it revealing and so, as Jesus breaks the bread, with the same hands that have been nailed to a cross, Cleopas recognizes him. All this time Cleopas and his companion have been hearing Jesus' story from the horse's mouth, yet it isn't until the breaking of bread that they realize who they're with. Some translations talk about scales falling from their eyes, allowing them to see Jesus.

I think it's something to do with the brokenness. Verse 35 makes the point that they recognized him because he broke the bread in the same way he did the night before his crucifixion. I don't think I could trust a God who hadn't, through Jesus, experienced something of human pain. I couldn't trust him with the pain of mental illness if I didn't know that he'd experienced the heaviest burden ever carried.

This passage also tells us a great deal about the way in which we can approach pastoral care. It has to be done in community and it has to be led from the pulpit. Biblical preaching not only engages with the text but also analyses and expounds that text to highlight the issues that the reader may face, spanning the whole spectrum of life experience from joy and elation to despair and doubt. For example, in an Easter preaching series we might take time to focus on the despair of Jesus in Gethsemane; in a Christmas series we could look at Mary's fear alongside her willingness to serve the Lord.

It is the friends who have walked with us in moments of elation and desperation who are the ones we often hold most dear. And there is no greater example of this than Jesus, who holds us dear in every season of life.

5   Learning to breathe

If my first year at uni was one of discovery and my second was one of grief, my third year offered something of a resolution. It was said to us right at the beginning of freshers' week that Bible college builds your faith, deconstructs your faith and then allows you to rebuild it, hopefully with more knowledge and more heart, to create something far stronger.

This was certainly true of my third year. In some ways it was incredibly painful – the foreboding sense of an ending and the fear of what was to come – but in others it was filled with joy because for the first time in many years, I was happy. I could see that I wasn't the same person I had been when I first walked through the doors at 19, hiding my battle scars and unsure if life was for me.

I enjoyed the happiness, even if there was a lurking fear – a fear that the darkness would return, a fear that days would once again become lost in my 'sad eyes'. It was, though, a very useful fear in many ways – it kept me tethered to the ground and thankful for what I had, enabling me to use the happiness in the right way, while also preventing me from ever taking the light for granted.

I wasn't naive enough to think that I would never face darkness again – but I was granted the feel of the light and I liked it. So while life might once more become dark, I hoped and prayed that I could hold on to the hope of the light.

Life was good – and I was determined to enjoy the light and give glory to the one who had spoken the light into being.

As 2012 dawned, I felt that I was beginning to understand what recovery was and that I might possibly be experiencing it. I'd not self-harmed for almost a year and my studies were beginning to help me make sense of who I was, what I'd been through and where God had been in the midst of it. It was a fragile state, but it gave me hope that the past three years had been a foretaste of life to come, rather than a brief reprieve.

For the past year I'd been running mental health prayer sessions every week and as I thought about what was going to lie beyond graduation, I felt I was being called to keep going with ThinkTwice and my work on mental health awareness. I blogged every week as I explored what the Bible had to say about mental health and what it means for us in our churches. I began to dream about ThinkTwice moving beyond my Cath Kidston-covered uni bedroom and into churches filled with the mentally ill. I still wasn't sure what it was going to look like in the wild, but I was sure I wanted it there.

I'd decided to stay on at university to complete a research master's, and I excitedly compiled a proposal to study a contemporary pastoral theology of clinical depression. It felt like a natural progression from my undergraduate work – and I wanted to better understand the beast that had haunted my life for nearly eight years. My eyes were firmly fixed on the future: on moving in with a friend in North London, on the sale of my childhood home and Mum moving to a new town, on postgraduate study and making something out of ThinkTwice.

The day I finished my degree was warm and sunny, everything I had imagined it would be. I left my final exam feeling that I'd done my best and with a sense of wonder at how I'd reached that place after everything that had gone before. I skipped down the main stairs to the field and met two of my friends. We sat watching the clock until 4 p.m., the official finish of the exam, and then walked up to the library where the bell lived. According to LST tradition, the ringing of the bell is a rite of passage that marks the end of a degree. I walked up the stairs of the library feeling giddy; I had done it!

A week before graduation, I was told that I was going to receive the Commitment Prize for my year group. This was, I felt, a prize for sheer bloody-mindedness, but it felt significant. Regardless of how I did in my actual degree I couldn't comprehend how far God had brought the cereal-eating girl who had arrived three years before. A week later at graduation I turned to hear the cheers of my classmates, friends and family. I was overwhelmed with thankfulness that I had stayed and not run away as I had wanted to, and that I had actually achieved getting a degree.

The lessons I'd learned at college went far above and beyond the ones I learned in the lecture rooms, and as I prepared to leave and looked back on where I'd been, what kept returning to me was something I'd begun to realize at 14.

When I'd first become ill, and started searching desperately through the Bible for some comfort, the passage I returned to again and again was Romans 8. It had spoken to me so powerfully throughout the intervening years. Paul was well and truly broken, wasn't he? A man of strength broken by God so that he could be God's man.

Paul knew about pain, and that's why I trust this passage in Romans so much. Verse 18, if I'm honest, used to annoy me quite intensely: 'I consider that the sufferings of this present time are not worth comparing with the glory about to be revealed in us.'

Thanks, really helpful. It seems glib, a get-out clause for God, when we first read it. And then we remember what Paul had been through – he's not talking from a life without pain. Most of the letters of Paul included in our Bible are written from a prison cell. Paul is not diminishing the suffering we share in life; he's saying that the suffering, although great, is nothing compared to glory that is to come.

Nor is he saying that suffering is a prerequisite to glory. He is setting out a vision for something so beautiful and so indescribable that our pain can't compare.

It's hope.

Hope is mentioned six times in this short passage – Paul's trying to tell us something, I think. And he needs to be persistent about it, because hope is one of the first casualties of pain, and certainly of depression. Depression tears through our hope, exposing nothing but the regrets of the past and fear of the future. Even the things we know to be true can be dressed up as lies in depression. As Jeff Lucas writes in his book *Faith in the Fog*, 'Logic is often one of the first casualties when depression descends.'[1]

Depression blinds us to the promise Paul sets out in the next few verses, that 'the creation itself will be set free from its bondage to decay and will obtain the freedom of the glory of the children of God.' It's life that fades away when depression pushes itself to the fore. The bondage to decay becomes all-consuming.

My bondage to decay was very real. 'Decay' is a word rarely used in relation to suicide, but I'd argue it's very apt.

Suicide is bondage to decay. There is no consolation or solace in suicide, not really. Not for the individual and not for those left behind. Yet in the midst of the blackest night, God shows up – and that is where we get our liberation from. Paul doesn't say here that we will be liberated from the hard stuff in life, but he does give us a vision of eternity.

Paul goes on to say, 'Hope that is seen is not hope. For who hopes for what is seen?' How right! I can hope for a healed mind – but I don't hope for a driving licence. I have one of those!

So often we dare not hope for what life on earth could look like, let alone for what eternal life could look like. Our hope, like our bodies, is fragile. So God gave us his Spirit. The Spirit is our foretaste of heaven and our comfort. Verse 26 says, 'In the same way, the Spirit helps us in our weakness, for we do not know how to pray as we ought, but that very Spirit intercedes with sighs too deep for words.'

It is an intercessionary Spirit that groans on our behalf when there are no words for the pain. It is a Spirit that doesn't always remove the pain but, rather, makes it 'creatively bearable', as in the case of the thorn in Paul's side. It is moreover a reminder for those of us who deliver pastoral care that we aren't in heaven yet. We experience the pain and frustrations of a fallen world – but we have the hope of heaven.

Theologian Frank Lake describes in the following way a biblical mandate for the delivery of pastoral care: 'The nature of the help God gives through His Church is to make what cannot be removed creatively bearable. Paul's thorn in the flesh remained . . . Resting in the power of God, he could glory his infirmity.'[2]

It's our task to make that which may not be healed until a new creation is heralded not only bearable but also fruitful, demonstrating the power and the love of God through the weakness and pain of humankind just as God did when he sent his Son to die on a sinner's cross.

As my glorious, sun-filled graduation day drew to a close, I thought about the three wonderful, weird, painful and challenging years that I had spent at LST. It had been one of the best days of my life and the pictures taken at the service show that I smiled ecstatically throughout most of it!

I managed to cry only once – and that was when I left the room that had been my home for the last time. I had accessorized in that room, covered it in Cath Kidston, laughed, cried, studied and socialized in it – and as I was leaving it, and I slid the white piece of paper with my name on it from the sign on the door, I knew this was it.

Hours earlier, as I had walked up the steps to shake the hands of both the principal and then the president of LST, I heard the cheers of my classmates and looked out at my family.

Graduation reminded me how far I was now from the scared, scarred young girl who stepped through the doors three years before. I still got scared, I still carried scars, but I was getting better. Graduation, for me at least, marked something else. It marked my survival, when so often I'd felt I couldn't go on.

I had certainly not been alone in that feeling. Indeed, many of my classmates had fought the kind of battles that hadn't featured even in my nightmares. We all arrived with our own baggage.

I think many of us now felt that, even if that baggage hadn't disappeared or lightened, it had changed shape.

Because we had all changed shape. I couldn't think of a single member of my class who hadn't changed for the better over the past three years. Above all, graduation day reminded me of God's amazing transformative power.

God transforms. He transforms through his word. Through his Church. Through his Spirit. Through his people.

His people showed me the love, the grace and the oh so gentle shoves of God. What strikes me most thinking about it now is that for the first time I was hopeful. After what felt like a lifetime of struggling for air, I could breathe – and I wanted to continue to breathe in God's Spirit. Right from our first breath in Genesis, God's breath has given us life and it continues to sustain us. When so often I have felt like depression is walking among the dead, I'm reminded by the passage in Ezekiel that speaks of God breathing life into dry bones. It's the same word, *ruah*, which can mean breath, spirit or wind. The breath of God is his Spirit and that is what gives life at every stage.

Ezekiel 37 says, 'Then he said to me, "Prophesy to these bones and say to them, Dry bones, hear the word of the LORD! This is what the Sovereign LORD says to these bones: I will make breath enter you, and you will come to life."'

It's a picture of the desperation and hopelessness of exile, of the separation between the northern tribes and Judah, but for me it speaks of the desperation and hopelessness of mental illness. Through Ezekiel's prophetic words, God is calling his people from death to life, from disharmony to unity. It's a foreshadowing of the hope of resurrection, which is to come through Jesus. God speaks of giving breath and giving life, and in the New Testament we see Jesus continuing this restoration.

John 20.21 records, 'Again Jesus said, "Peace be with you! As the Father has sent me, I am sending you." With that, he breathed on them and said, "Receive the Holy Spirit."'[3] The breath of God renews, unifies and heals right through Scripture, and when mental illness leaves us languishing in the graveyard of life, God's breath restores us.

I have experienced great healing, yet it hasn't resulted in the removal of my diagnosis. I still need to take my antidepressant medication, but it is a healing nonetheless because I've found that there is life to be lived even in the darkest mists of mental illness. I'm not breathing completely freely – but I'm not struggling to breathe either. I'm just learning to breathe every day.

Matt Bays beautifully describes what this healing feels like: 'Sometimes it feels as if God has invited himself into my pain, when I had hoped to be invited into his healing. We want a God who heals our wounds, but it seems we have a God who heals our hearts.'[4]

I find God in my mental illness and I find God in my pain.

I find him to be present perhaps most often in the people who have loved me at my darkest, who have persisted in their friendship towards and love of me when I've been at my most unlovable. Mental illness often doesn't make people the best patients. I've pushed away the ones who love me the most, tried to hide the glaringly obvious struggle and lashed out when I've felt cornered, yet they have stayed. They've hugged me and prayed on my behalf when I couldn't speak through my tears, and again and again I've glimpsed something of the character of

God through them. As I explained it recently, I was loved back to life and the land of the living. The God who loves his prodigal children goes further than we can imagine to call us back to him.

I've also found him in the Church: the broken, imperfect but impossibly beautiful representation of the kingdom of God on earth. Throughout my life I've been a member of three churches, each wonderful in its own way and each imperfect. The first was the one that nurtured the shoot of my faith and encouraged me to tend it myself; it was where I first discovered a love of preaching and singing. The second was a home from home while I was at university, cheering me on as I searched for my calling. The third is the one I now call home. I visited it once and I've not yet left. It's the church I met and married my husband in; it's office is where ThinkTwice operates out of; and it's the place where I've had the muscles of my faith and my calling stretched.

The Church has a vital role to play in mental health care, not only in terms of individual pastoral care but also in the way we approach the matter in our preaching and corporate worship. The inclusion of mental health conditions in our intercessory prayers is a simple way to ensure that we aren't ignoring mental and emotional health. The primary way this can be done is through the Bible. I cannot stress too highly the importance of engaging with the emotions of the passages we preach; the biblical characters we know so well weren't robots, and to ignore their emotions is to miss the point of God giving us a Bible whose stories show him working through people's lives.

All too often, I see the words of the Bible misused – encouragements become condemnations and words that were meant to bring hope bring nothing but despair. One of the most common misconceptions is that depression in Christians is not allowed because it says in Nehemiah 8.10, 'the joy of the LORD is your strength'. The verse was first and foremost written for the people of God as they wept over the reading of the laws that convicted them of their sins; the command not to grieve was a marker to the people that their time of repentance was over. The reason for their grief had passed, and now was the time to celebrate what God had done for them.

When we apply verses like this one to depression without thought for its context, we miss the point. The joy of the Lord is our strength, and this is as true during depression as it is during the rest of life. Sometimes, though, as Timothy Keller writes, 'the joy of the Lord happens inside the sorrow.'[5] Joy is not happiness in the same way that depression is not sadness. Joy goes above and beyond a fleeting smile, because it's the promise of our salvation. As Calvin Miller writes: 'Many Christians confuse happiness with joy, as did I. Happiness is about a buoyant emotion that results from the momentary plateaus of well-being that characterize our lives. Joy, however, is bedrock stuff. Joy is a confidence that operates irrespective of our moods.'[6]

Joy and depression aren't mutually exclusive – it's possible to hold fast to the promise of salvation and be sure of it in the midst of the deepest depression. Throughout the decade in which I was most unwell, I didn't question the existence of God or the story of Scripture. At times I questioned his character, but for the most part I was as sure of my own salvation as anyone is.

Finding happiness can't be the aim of our lives, otherwise we will more often than not be disappointed. Finding joy is about finding God and through him experiencing something of the shalom I spoke about earlier in the book. As I've been learning to breathe, the concept of shalom has been one of the most helpful

I've found to enable me to live life to the full, because it's a vision for hope.

One day everyone will eat and drink without worrying where it's come from or how many calories it contains. Our work will be fulfilling rather than futile, we will appreciate the beauty of the world around us without also being witness to its decay, our relationships won't be broken and we will be safe in our minds and in our bodies.

It's a vision of heaven and of hope that I look to on the darkest days, but it's also one that through God's Spirit we can glimpse here on earth. It's what learning to breathe has been about for me; not a life that is free from all pain and shame, but a life in which I find God at work in me, in the stories I hear and in the lives of those around me.

Epilogue

As I've been writing this book I have been able to see where God was at work and yet I missed him. I've opened my teenage diary to jog my memory for the parts of my story that I'd forgotten. It was strange reading the words of a girl who didn't know what was happening to her, who couldn't understand her tears, yet also wrote about fancying unobtainable boys and friendship squabbles. The two sit side by side in this diary – the teenage trials of first loves and homework next to the confusion and desperation caused by the depression that forced itself into my life.

I'm very glad I wrote the diary; it's made my job as a writer much easier. It's also a wonderful chance to look back through the pages of my life and see God's handwriting alongside my own.

It wasn't easy to look back at the hardest and most painful times of my life, but there is something particularly beautiful about seeing Jesus move on every page, staying my hand and holding hope before me.

As I look back through the pages written in those darkest years, I see the Light of the World shining when I couldn't see it and couldn't understand it. Where then I could see only glimpses, now I'm hit with the force of God's light through my story.

Writing this book has been an adventure. It has hurt and it

has been healing. Perhaps the most difficult part was writing to others to hear their memories of me at my darkest. It was also the most encouraging, because they revealed that even as I perched precariously between life and death, they believed in my ability to live and to make something out of the darkness I'd lived through.

Their hope and faith that the God who had brought me this far would bring me through was something they reflected back to me as they fought with me and for me during those years.

I believe it's important for us to learn our own stories, because in learning them we can see what we otherwise might have missed – that in our most desperate darkness God doesn't abandon us because, through Jesus, he experienced the ultimate desolation on the cross.

No heartbreak we face, whether caused by mental illness or otherwise, is alien to God, because Jesus experienced the greatest agony in human history. In my darkest hours, hours when it sometimes felt like the darkness would kill me, I have found my hope in the God who is light, 'the light of all mankind. The light shines in the darkness, and the darkness has not overcome it.'

The darkness of Jesus' crucifixion couldn't quench the light and love of God, and neither can any darkness we face ourselves.

As I mentioned right at the start, this wasn't the book I intended to write. When I was 15 I couldn't even say the words 'self-harm' and hardly anyone around me knew the extent of my mental illness as a teenager, but over the past decade I've come to see that when we share our stories we can't help but share something of God.

Throughout my story – through all the locust years, the times I so nearly ended it all, through the endless tears and the snatches of solace – I've seen God moving in my life.

My story isn't extraordinary, but the God of my story is.

Appendix

The mental health charity Mind describes some of the common symptoms of clinical depression as set out below.

How you might feel	How you might behave
• down, upset or tearful • restless, agitated or irritable • guilty, worthless and down on yourself • empty and numb • isolated and unable to relate to other people • finding no pleasure in life or things you usually enjoy • a sense of unreality • no self-confidence or self-esteem • hopeless and despairing • suicidal	• avoiding social events and activities you usually enjoy • self-harming or suicidal behaviour • finding it difficult to speak or think clearly • losing interest in sex • difficulty in remembering or concentrating on things • using more tobacco, alcohol or other drugs than usual • difficulty sleeping or sleeping too much • feeling tired all the time • no appetite and losing weight or eating too much and gaining weight • physical aches and pains with no obvious physical cause • moving very slowly or being restless and agitated

Resources

Anorexia & Bulimia Care

Saville Court

10–11 Saville Place

Clifton

Bristol BS8 4EJ

Tel.: 03000 11 12 13 (helpline)

Website: www.anorexiabulimiacare.org.uk

A Christian organization providing information for carers and support for individuals with eating disorders.

Association of Christian Counsellors

29 Momus Boulevard

Coventry CV2 5NA

Tel.: 0845 124 9569

Website: www.acc-uk.org

A professional body that aims to ensure quality counselling and pastoral care, it has a directory of national, regional and local Christian counsellors.

Mental Health Access Pack

Website: www.mentalhealthaccesspack.org

Livability, the Mind and Soul Foundation and Premier Life have teamed up to provide this free resource that aims to educate, encourage and enable churches to support those with mental health issues.

Mind and Soul

Website: www.mindandsoulfoundation.org

A website that aims to educate, encourage and equip the Church to engage theology with contemporary scientific mental health care.

Premier Lifeline

22 Chapter Street

London SW1P 4NP

Tel.: 0300 111 0101 (helpline 9 a.m.–12 p.m.)

Website: www.premierlifeline.org.uk

A Christian website that also has a helpline (see above), offering a listening ear, prayer and signposting.

tastelife

Tel.: 07845 089 400

Website: www.tastelifeuk.org

An eating disorders organization that offers a community education course, training and information.

ThinkTwice

Website: www.thinktwiceinfo.org

A charity founded by Rachael Newham to create awareness of mental health issues in the Church and offer training and consultancy nationwide.

OTHER ORGANIZATIONS

Beat

Unit 1 Chalk Hill House

19 Rosary Road

Norwich

Norfolk NR1 1SZ

Tel.: 0808 801 0677 (adult helpline 3 p.m.–10 p.m.)

0808 801 0711 (youthline 3 p.m.–10 p.m.)

0808 801 0811 (studentline 3 p.m.–10 p.m.)

Website: www.beateatingdisorders.org.uk

A national charity providing information on eating disorders, plus support groups and professional training.

Mind

15–19 Broadway

Stratford

London E15 4BQ

Tel.: 0300 123 3393 (infoline)

Website: www.mind.org.uk

A national charity providing advice and support for those with mental illness and their families.

Rethink

Tel.: 0300 5000 927 (advice and information)

Website: www.rethink.org

Provides expert advice to those affected by mental illness as well as support groups.

Samaritans

Freepost RSRB-KKBY-CYJK

PO Box 9090

Stirling FK8 2SA

Tel.: 116 123

Website: www.samaritans.org

Operates a 24/7 helpline, informative website with online help and provides a listening service.

ORGANIZATIONS WORKING WITH YOUNG PEOPLE

Papyrus

Lineva House

28–32 Milner Street

Warrington

Cheshire WA5 1AD

Tel.: 0800 068 41 41

Website: www.papyrus-uk.org

A national charity working to prevent suicide in young people by offering confidential support and training.

YoungMinds

Tel.: 0808 802 5544 (parents' helpline 9.30 a.m.–4 p.m.)

Website: www.youngminds.org.uk

A national charity that offers helplines and information.

Youthscape

Bute Mills

74 Bute Street

Luton LU1 2EY

Tel.: 01582 877220

Website: www.youthscape.co.uk

A Christian organization that works locally with young people in Luton, but also provides national resources via selfharmUK, Romance Academy and schoolsworkuk.

Notes

2 STRUGGLING FOR AIR

1 Swinton, J. (2001) *Spirituality and Mental Health Care*. London: Jessica Kingsley Publishers. P. 95.

2 Wilkinson, J. (1980) *Health and Healing*. Edinburgh: Handsel Press. P. 5.

3 www.who.int/features/factfiles/mental_health/en> (accessed February 2018).

4 Wurtzel, E. (2014) *Prozac Nation: Young and depressed in America*. Houghton Mifflin Harcourt. P. 179.

5 Brueggeman, W. (2005) *The Message of the Psalms*. Minneapolis: Augsberg Press. P. 78.

3 SUFFOCATION

1 www.mdedge.com/currentpsychiatry/article/80610/depression/passive-suicidal-ideation-still-high-risk-clinical (accessed February 2018).

2 Hornbacher, M. (2005) *Wasted: A memoir of anorexia and bulimia*. London: HarperCollins. P. 123.

3 Epperly, B. (2001) 'Living through Holy Saturday', *Patheos*, 15 April, 2011.

4 Rambo, S. (2010) *Spirit and Trauma*. Louisville: John Knox Press. P. 7.

4 RESUSCITATION

1 Swinton, J. (2007) *Raging with Compassion*. Cambridge, MA: Eerdmans. P. 102.

2 Vanier, J. and Swinton, J. (2014) *Mental Health: The inclusive church resource*. London: Darton, Longman & Todd. P. 70.

3 Billings, T. (2015) *Rejoicing in Lament*. Grand Rapids: Brazos Press. P. 17.

4 Nouwen, H. (2008) *The Wounded Healer*. London: Darton, Longman & Todd, P. 87.

5 LEARNING TO BREATHE

1 Lucas, J. (2013) *Faith in the Fog*. Grand Rapids: Zondervan. P. 128.

2 Lake, F. (2006) *Clinical Theology: A theological and psychiatric basis to clinical pastoral care*. Lexington: Emeth Press. P. xxv.

3 Pretlove, J. (2005) 'John 20:22 – help from dry bones?', *Criswell Theological Review*, September 3(1): 93–101.

4 Bays, M. (2016) *Finding God in the Ruins*. Colorado Springs: David C. Cook. P. 133.

5 Keller, T. (2015) *Walking with God Through Pain and Suffering*. London: Hodder & Stoughton. P. 253.

6 Miller, C. (1983) *Joy*. Downers Grove, IL: IVP. Pp. 10–11.